To Marni –
Love,
Brian

THE
STEWARD OF
CHRISTENDOM

BY SEBASTIAN
BARRY

★

DRA~
PLAY

10/02

First produced at the Royal Court Upstairs on 30 March 1995
by Out of Joint and the Royal Court Theatre.

Subsequently produced at the Royal Court Downstairs on 7 September 1995
by Out of Joint and the Royal Court Theatre.

First produced in America at the Brooklyn Academy of Music, New York
on 19 January 1997 by Out of Joint.

THE STEWARD OF CHRISTENDOM received its premiere at the Royal Court Theatre Upstairs, in London, England, on March 30, 1995. It was directed by Max Stafford-Clark; the set design was by Julian McGowan; the costume design was by Jennifer Cook; the lighting design was by Johanna Town; original music was by Shaun Davey; the sound design was by Paul Arditti; and the stage managers were Rob Young, Sally McKenna, and Caroline Boocock. The cast was as follows:

THOMAS	Donal McCann
SMITH	Kieran Ahern
MRS. O'DEA	Maggie McCarthy
RECRUIT; MATT	Rory Murray
WILLIE	Jonathan Newman
ANNIE	Tina Kellegher
MAUD	Cara Kelly
DOLLY	Aislín McGuckin

THE STEWARD OF CHRISTENDOM was produced by Out of Joint Productions and the Brooklyn Academy of Music, at the Majestic Theater, in Brooklyn, New York, in January, 1997. It was directed by Max Stafford-Clark; the set and costume designs were by Julian McGowan; the lighting design was by Johanna Town; the music was by Shaun Davey; the sound design was by Paul Arditti; the production manager was Rob Young. The cast was as follows:

THOMAS	Donal McCann
SMITH	Kieran Ahern
MRS. O'DEA	Maggie McCarthy
RECRUIT; MATT	Rory Murray
WILLIE	Carl Brennan
ANNIE	Tina Kellegher
MAUD	Ali White
DOLLY	Aislín McGuckin

CHARACTERS

THOMAS DUNNE — early-to-mid seventies at the time of the play, 1932

SMITH — fiftyish

MRS. O'DEA — likewise or older

RECRUIT — eighteen

WILLIE DUNE — Thomas' son, born late 1890s, died in the First World War, thirteen or so as he appears in the play to Thomas, his voice not yet broken

ANNIE DUNNE — Thomas' middle daughter, bowed back, about twenty in 1922, thirtyish 1932

MAUD DUNNE — Thomas' eldest daughter, early twenties in 1922

DOLLY DUNNE — Thomas' youngest daughter, about seventeen in 1922

MATT KIRWIN — Maud's suitor and husband, mid-to-late twenties in 1922, mid-to-late thirties in 1932

The play is set in the county home in Baltinglass, County Wicklow, in about 1932.

THE STEWARD
OF CHRISTENDOM

ACT ONE

Circa 1932. Thomas' bare room in the county home in Balt-inglass. A toiling music-hall music distantly. A poor table, an iron bed with a thin mattress and yellowing sheets. A grey blanket, a three-legged stool. A poor patch of morning light across Thomas, a solitary man of seventy-five, in the bed. His accent is southwest Wicklow, with his words clear.

THOMAS.   Da Da, Ma Ma, Ba Ba, Ba Ba. Clover, clover in my mouth, clover honey-smelling, clover smelling of Ma Ma's neck, and Ma Ma's soft breast when she opens her floating blouse, and Da Da's bright boots in the grasses, amid the wild clover, and the clover again, and me the Ba Ba set in the waving grasses, and the smell of honey, and the farmhands going away like an army of redcoats but without the coats, up away up the headland with their scythes, and every bit of the sun likes to run along the scythes and laugh along the blades, now there are a score of shining scythes, dipping and signalling from the backs of the men. *(A sharp bang on the door.)*
SMITH.   Wakey, wakey!
THOMAS.   Who is there?
SMITH.   Black Jim. Black Jim in the morning.
THOMAS.   Oh, don't come in, Black Jim, with your black-thorn stick raised high.
SMITH.   It's Black Jim.
THOMAS.   But don't you come in. There's no need. Is it Da

Da?

SMITH. It's Black Jim, and he must come in.

THOMAS. There's no need. Thomas sleepy sleepy, beddy bye. Is it Da Da? *(No answer. More distantly on other doors there's a banging and the same "wakey, wakey" receding.)* Da Da comes in, Da Da comes in, Tom no sleepy, Tom no sleepy. Tom you sleep, says Da Da, or you get big stick. And when little Tom no sleepy sleep, big stick comes in and hitting Tom Tommy, but now the polished boots are gone, and the dark has closed over the fields, and the smell of the clover is damped down now by summer cold, and the dress of Ma Ma hangs on the chair, and her face is pressed into the goosey pillow, and all is silence in the wooden world of the house, except the tread of the Da Da, a-worrying, a-worrying, except the fall of the big stick, cut from the blackthorn tree in the hushed deeps of winter. Da Da is golden, golden, golden, nothing that Da Da do takes away the sheen and the swoon of gold. *(He bestirs himself, wipes his big hands on his face vigorously, gets out of bed with good strength. He is big-framed but diminished by age, in a not-too-clean set of long johns.)* You bloody mad old man. Gabbling and affrighting yourself in the dark. Baltinglass, Baltinglass, that's where you are. For your own good, safe from harm. Like the milking cow taken down from the sloping field when the frost begins to sit on her tail. When her shit is frosty. Snug in the byre. *(He sits on the stool and leans in to the table as if pressing his face against the cow.)* Come to it, Daisy now, give your milk. Go on. *(Slaps a leg.)* Ah, Daisy, Daisy, sweet, give it up, for Thomas. Oh. *(As if getting a jet into the bucket.)* Oh, oh. *(Happily.)* Aye. *(Catching himself, stopping.)* The county home in Baltinglass, that's where you're situated. Seventy-five summers on your head and mad as a stone mason. Safe, safe, safety, safe, safe, safety, mad as a barking stone mason. Because you were not civil to your daughter, no, you were not. You were ranting, you were raving, and so they put you where you were safe. Like a dog that won't work without using his teeth, like a dog under sentence. But please do not you talk to Black Jim, Thomas, please do not, there's the manny. Because he is not there. *(Singing.)* There was an old woman that lived in the wood, willa, willa, wallya. *(His own si-*

6

lence.) Da Da? (*Mrs. O'Dea, the seamstress, a small plump woman in an ill-made dress and a white apron with big pockets full of tape and needles and oddments of black cloth, opens the door with her key and comes in.*)

MRS. O'DEA. (*A local accent.*) Will you let me measure you today, Mr. Dunne?

THOMAS. What for indeed?

MRS. O'DEA. You can't wear those drawers forever.

THOMAS. I won't need to, Mrs. O'Dea, I won't live forever.

MRS. O'DEA. And what will you do when summer's gone? How can you bear to wear rags?

THOMAS. I rarely go out, you see.

MRS. O'DEA. Look at the state of yourself. You're like something in a music hall. Mrs. Forbes, the Boneless Wonder, or some such.

THOMAS. This is a madhouse, it suits me to look like a madman while I'm here.

MRS. O'DEA. If you allow me measure you, I'll make up a fine suit for you, as good as my own attire.

THOMAS. With that black cloth you use for all the poor men?

MRS. O'DEA. Yes and indeed, it must be black, by regulation of the board.

THOMAS. If you had a bit of gold or suchlike for the thread, something to perk the suit up, why then, Mrs. O'Dea, I would let you measure me.

MRS. O'DEA. Gold thread? I have none of that, Mr. Dunne.

THOMAS. That's my bargain. Take it or leave it.

MRS. O'DEA. Would a yellow do?

THOMAS. Yes, yes.

MRS. O'DEA. You're not afraid of looking like a big goose?

THOMAS. I go out but rarely. If I look like a goose, few will see me. (*As an inspiration.*) I won't venture out at Christmas!

MRS. O'DEA. (*Taking out her measuring tape.*) Have you fleas?

THOMAS. No, madam.

MRS. O'DEA. (*Calling out the door.*) Mr. Smith! (*To Thomas.*) You won't mind Mr. Smith washing you, just a little.

THOMAS. (*Anxiously.*) Don't let Black Jim in here. Don't let

7

him, for I've no sugar lumps. It's only sugar lumps appeases him.

MRS. O'DEA. He must wash you, Mr. Dunne. It's just Mr. Smith. You smell like a piece of pork left out of the dripping press, man dear. *(Smith, about fifty, balding, with the cheerfulness about him of the powerful orderly, comes in with a basin.)*

SMITH. Raise 'em.

THOMAS. *(Backing away)* The blackthorn stick hurts Tommy Tom. Sugar lumps, sugar lumps!

MRS. O'DEA. Take off your old long johns, and be easy in yourself. It's only a sponging.

THOMAS. *(Trying to hold his clothes fast.)* Tum tum tum, bum bum bum. *(Smith roughly unbuttons the long johns and pulls them off, Thomas miserably covering himself.)*

SMITH. I'd a mind once to join my brother on the Hudson River. He has a whale flensing business there, flourishing. Would that I had joined Jack, I say, when I have to wash down an old bugger like you. I would rather flense whales, and that's a stinking task, I'm told.

THOMAS. *(Smiling red-faced at Mrs. O'Dea.)* Da Da.

MRS. O'DEA. *(Smith beginning to sponge.)* Good man yourself, Mr. Dunne.

THOMAS. *(Weeping.)* Da Da, Ma Ma, Ba Ba.

MRS. O'DEA. My, my, that's a fine chest you have on you, Mr. Dunne. What was your work formerly? I know you've told me often enough.

THOMAS. *(Proudly enough.)* I was a policeman.

MRS. O'DEA. You had the chest for it.

THOMAS. I had, madam.

SMITH. *(Sponging.)* Dublin Metropolitan Police, weren't you, boyo? In your braid. The DMP, that are no more. Oh, la-di-da. Look at you.

THOMAS. *(Smiling oddly.)* La-di-da.

SMITH. *(Sponging.)* Castle Catholic bugger that you were. But you're just an old bastard in here with no one to sponge you but Smith.

THOMAS. Black Jim no like Tommy Tom. No like Tommy Tom.

SMITH. Chief superintendent, this big gobshite was, Mrs. O'Dea, that killed four good men and true in O'Connell Street in the days of the lock-out. Larkin. Hah? His men it was struck down the strikers. *(A gentle hit with the drying cloth.)* Baton-charging. A big loyal Catholic gobshite killing poor hungry Irishmen. If you weren't an old madman we'd flay you.

MRS. O'DEA. That's fine, Mr. Smith, leave him be. Can't you see you terrorise him? That's him scrubbed.

SMITH. *(Going off with the basin.)* Excusing my language.

MRS. O'DEA. Can you put on your own clothes, Mr. Dunne?

THOMAS. I can, madam.

MRS. O'DEA. Is it true you gave your previous suit to a man in the walking meadow?

THOMAS. It is. *(Dressing.)*

MRS. O'DEA. Why would you do a thing like that, and go in those rags yourself? Was the man you gave it to cold?

THOMAS. No. He was hungry.

MRS. O'DEA. There's no eating in a suit, man dear.

THOMAS. I was out a-walking in the lunatics' meadow, and Patrick O'Brien asked me for the suit. He was in former times the finest thrower of the bullet in Kiltegan. Do you know what a bullet is? It is a ball of granite whittled down in an evening by a boy. I could tell you tales of Patrick O'Brien and the bullet, on the roads there round about. All the men of the village milling there, raging to win fame at the bulleting if God shone the light of luck on them, the thrower slowly slowly raising the bullet, slowly dipping it, then away, with a great fling of the arm, down the road with it, and well beyond the next corner if he could. And if the bullet touched the grassy marge, a terrible groan would issue from the man and his supporters. And the young boys red in the face from ambition and desire. Patrick O'Brien, a tall yellow streak of a man now, that thinks he is a dog. A dog, Mrs. O'Dea. When he asked for the suit, I couldn't refuse him, for memory of his great skill. They were evenings any human person would remember.

MRS. O'DEA. *(Measuring him now with the tape, putting up his arms and so on as necessary.)* What did he want with your suit?

THOMAS. To eat, he said. To bury it and eat it, piecemeal,

9

as the spirit took him.

MRS. O'DEA.   You gave your good suit to a poor madman to be eaten?

THOMAS.   I was glad to give it to him. Though indeed truly, it was one of Harrison's suits, and the last of my finery from the old days. A nice civilian suit, made by Harrison, in North Great George's Street, years ago.

MRS. O'DEA.   I can't believe that you gave away a suit like that. A lovely bespoke suit.

THOMAS.   Why not? Amn't I a lunatic myself?

MRS. O'DEA.   (Sensibly.) Well, there must be a year's eating in a man's suit. You won't need to give him the new one.

THOMAS.   No, but it won't be much to me all the same, if it has no gold in it. The boy that sings to me betimes wears gold, and I have a hankering now for a suit with a touch of gold. There was never enough gold in that uniform. If I had made commissioner I might have had gold, but that wasn't a task for a Catholic, you understand, in the way of things, in those days.

MRS. O'DEA.   You must have been a fine policeman, if they made you all of a chief superintendent.

THOMAS.   Maybe so. But, to tell you the truth, I was forty-five years in the DMP when they did so, and promotion was really a matter of service. Not that they would put a fool to such a task, when you think of the terrible responsibility of it. I had three-hundred men in B Division, and kept all the great streets and squares of Dublin orderly and safe, and was proud, proud to do it well.

MRS. O'DEA.   I am sure you did, Mr. Dunne, because you carry yourself well yet. You mustn't mind Mr. Smith. He's younger than yourself and one of his brothers was shot in the twenties, so he tells me.

THOMAS.   The DMP was never armed, not like the Royal Irish Constabulary. The RIC could go to war. That's why we were taken off the streets during that rebellion at Easter time, that they make so much of now. We were mostly country men, and Catholics to boot, and we loved our King and we loved our country. They never put those Black and Tans among us, because we were a force that belonged to Dublin and her streets.

10

We did our best and followed our orders. Go out to Mount Jerome some day, in the city of Dublin, and see the old monument to the DMP men killed in the line of duty. Just ordinary country men keen to do well. And when the new government came in, they treated us badly. Our pensions were in disarray. Some said we had been traitors to Ireland. Though we sat in Dublin Castle all through twenty-two and tried to protect the city while the whole world was at each other's throats. While the most dreadful and heinous murders took place in the fields of Ireland. With nothing but our batons and our pride. Maybe we weren't much. You're thinking, of course he would speak well for his crowd. Yes, I'll speak well for them. We were part of a vanished world, and I don't know what's been put in our place. I'd live to see them clear Sackville Street of an illegal gathering without breaking a few heads. There was a proclamation posted the week before that meeting. It was my proper duty to clear the thoroughfare. There was no one killed that day that I know of, there were scores of my men in Jervis Street and the like, with head wounds. I'm sorry Smith's brother was killed. I'm sorry for all the poor souls killed these last years. Let them come and kill me if they wish. But I know my own story of what happened, and I am content with it.

MRS. O'DEA.   Mercy, Mr. Dunne, I didn't mean to prompt a declaration. You're all in a sweat, man. The sooner you have a new suit, the better.

THOMAS.   But I tell you, there's other things I regret, and I regret them sorely, things of my own doing, and damn history.

MRS. O'DEA.   We all have our regrets, man dear. Do calm yourself.

THOMAS.   I regret that day with my daughter Annie and the sword, when we were home and snug in Kiltegan at last.

MRS. O'DEA.   There, there, man dear. We'll see if we can't keep the next suit on you, when you go a-walking in the lunatics' meadow, as you call it. It's just the exercise field, you know, the walking meadow. It will have plenty of yellow in it.

THOMAS.   *(Differently, head down.)* I suppose it is very sad about Patrick O'Brien. I suppose.

MRS. O'DEA.   I have all your measurements now, Mr. Dunne.

11

And a fine big-boned gentleman you are. *(Looking at his bare feet.)* What became of your shoes, but?

MRS. O'DEA and THOMAS. *(After a moment, as one.)* Patrick O'Brien!

MRS. O'DEA. Maybe there's a pair of decent shoes about in the cupboards, that someone has left.

THOMAS. Coffin shoes, you mean, I expect. Oh, I don't mind a dead man's shoes. And a nice suit, yes, that I can wear in my own coffin, to match, with yellow thread.

MRS. O'DEA. Not yet, Mr. Dunne, not by a long chalk. *(Going out.)* I'll do my best for you. *(Locking the door.)*

THOMAS. *(Alone, in an old summer light.)* When the rain of autumn started that year, my mother and me went down into the valley by the green road. Myself trotting beside her in my boyish joy. We passed the witch's farm, where the witch crossed the fields in her dirty dress to milk her bloodied cow, that gave her bloodied milk, a thing to fear because she used the same well as ourselves, and washed her bucket there before drawing water. My father was the steward of Humewood and she should have feared to hurt our well, but you cannot withstand the mad. Well, we passed the nodding bell-flowers that I delighted to burst, and ventured out on to the Baltinglass road, to beg a perch for our bums on a cart. *(Sitting up on the bedstead.)* For my father would not let my mother take the pony and trap, because he said the high lamps made too great a show of pride, and we were proud people enough without having to show it. Not that he didn't drive the trap himself when he needed. But we were soon in the old metropolis of Baltinglass, a place of size and wonder to a boy. *(Pulling out his ragged socks from under the mattress.)* There we purchased a pair of lace-up boots. A pair of lace-up boots which banished bare feet, which I was soon able to lace and tighten for myself of a morning, when the air in the bedroom was chill as a well, and the icy cock crowed in the frosty yard, and Thomas Dunne was young and mightily shod. *(Looking down at his feet.)* And Dolly my daughter later polished my policeman's boots, and Annie and Maud brought me my clothes brushed and starched in the mornings, as the castle of soldiers and constables woke. When my poor wife was

12

dead those many years, and Little Ship Street stirred with the milkman's cart. And the sun herself brought gold to the river's back. *(He looks at the locked door.)* If they lock that door how can my daughters come to rescue me? *(He holds out a hand and takes it with his other hand, and shakes.)* How do you do? How do you do? *(Very pleased.)* How do you do? *(Holds out his arms, embraces someone.)* How do you do? *(Gently.)* How do you do? Oh, how do you do? *(Music. After a little, Smith enters with a cracked bowl with a steam of stew off it. He hands Thomas a big spoon which Thomas holds obediently.)*

SMITH. You look just like an old saint there, Mr. Dunne, an old saint there, with your spoon. You may think me a rough sort of man but I know my saints. I seen a picture of St. Jerome with a spoon like that and a bowl like that. *(Thomas sits to eat.)* Eat away, man. You should see the cauldron of that stuff the cooks have made. The kitchens are in a fog. Seven lambs went into it, they say. Isn't it good stuff? *(Friendly.)* What's it your name is again, your first name? I've so many to remember.

THOMAS. Thomas. They named me Thomas long ago for my great-great-grandfather the first steward of Humewood, the big place in Kiltegan, the main concern. Though all his own days they called him White Meg on account of his fierce white beard. He'd stride up the old street from his house to the great gates and say nothing to no one. White Meg. But Thomas it was, was his name.

SMITH. With your spoon. St. Thomas! When I brought Mrs. O'Dea her cocoa in at five, she had you all cut out and hung up on a hook with the other inhabitants, and the breeze was blowing you softly from the crack in the pane. She's a keen seamstress. St. Thomas. Do you like the stew?

THOMAS. *(Expansively.)* Of all the dishes in the world I may say I relish mostly a stew.

SMITH. You, St. Thomas, that knew kings and broke Larkin. Stew.

THOMAS. *(Alerted.)* Put a piece of lamb in it at the bottom, for the men that are working, and let the child eat off the top of it. The child's spoon is a shallow spoon. Parsnips. The secret of stew on our hillside was just a scrape of crab apple in it —

13

just a scrape. But then we'd fierce crab apples. And not to curse while it was cooking. And not to spit while it was cooling.

SMITH. What was the name of the patriot was killed years past in Thomas Street outside the church of St. Thomas, in the city of Dublin?

THOMAS. *(Thinking, innocently.)* Thomas Street wasn't in my division. But Emmet, was it, you mean? Robert Emmet?

SMITH. That's the one. They hung him there and the people cried out against the soldiers and the peelers, and after they dragged his body over the parade ground till it was bleeding and broken in its bones, and then they got a loyal butcher to cut him into four pieces. He was dead then.

THOMAS. I should think.

SMITH. That's what they did to him, those official men, and a fine Protestant gentleman at that.

THOMAS. *(Pleasantly.)* It's as well to throw a bit of rosemary across it too, if you have rosemary. Rosemary smells good when the land gets hot. Across the stew. Rosemary. Thyme would do either, if you've none. When you put in the spuds. Or lavender maybe. Did you ever try clover? A child will eat clover when he is set down on the meadow to sit. The bee's favourite. A cow makes fine milk from a field of clover. So put in rosemary, if you have it. Ah, fresh spuds, turned out of the blessed earth like — for all the world like newborn pups. *(Laughing.)*

SMITH. I suppose you held the day of Emmet's death as a festive day. A victory day. I suppose you did. I suppose you were all very queer indeed up there in the Castle. I'm thinking too of the days when they used to put the pitch caps on the priests when they catched them, like they were only dogs, and behind the thick walls of the city hall all the English fellas would be laughing at the screams of the priests, while their brains boiled. I'm thinking of all that. I suppose you never put a pitch cap on anyone. They weren't in fashion in your time. A pity. It must have been a great sight, all the same.

THOMAS. *(Eating rapidly.)* Good stew, good stew. Wicklow lambs.

SMITH. *(Looking at him.)* St. Thomas, isn't it?

THOMAS. *(Smiling.)* St. Thomas. *(Smith goes off with the empty bowl.)* I loved her for as long as she lived, I loved her as much as I loved Cissy my wife, and maybe more, or differently. When she died it was difficult to go from her to the men that came after her, Edward and George, they were good men but it was not the same. When I was a young recruit it used to frighten me how much I loved her. Because she had built everything up and made it strong, and made it shipshape. The great world that she owned was shipshape as a ship. All the harbours of the earth were trim with their granite piers, the ships were shining and strong. The trains went sleekly through the fields, and her mark was everywhere, Ireland, Africa, the Canadas, every blessed place. And men like me were there to make everything peaceable, to keep order in her kingdoms. She was our pride. Among her emblems was the gold harp, the same harp we wore on our helmets. We were secure, as if for eternity the orderly milk-drays would come up the streets in the morning, and her influence would reach everywhere, like the salt sea pouring up into the fresh waters of the Liffey. Ireland was hers for eternity, order was everywhere, if we could but honour her example. She loved her Prince. I loved my wife. The world was a wedding of loyalty, of steward to Queen, she was the very flower and perfecter of Christendom. Even as the simple man I was I could love her fiercely. Victoria. *(The Recruit, a young man of eighteen or so, comes on. He has obviously made a great effort to smarten himself for this meeting. He is tall and broad, and stoops a little as he takes off his hat.)* Good morning, son. How are you?

RECRUIT. Oh, most pleasant, sir, most pleasant.

THOMAS. You had a good journey up from your home place?

RECRUIT. It didn't take a feather out of me, sir.

THOMAS. Good man. What age are you?

RECRUIT. Eighteen, sir, this November past.

THOMAS. Height?

RECRUIT. Six foot three, sir, in my winter socks.

THOMAS. Well, you look a very fine man indeed. You were never in trouble yourself, son?

RECRUIT. Oh, no, sir.

THOMAS. And did you serve in the Great War? I don't sup-

15

pose you could have.

RECRUIT. No, sir. I was too young.

THOMAS. Of course. A soldier doesn't always make a good policeman. There's too much — sorrow — in a soldier. You're a drinking man?

RECRUIT. I'll drink a glass of porter, with my father.

THOMAS. Very good. I've read your father's letter. And I want to tell you, we are going to give you a go at it. I have a big book in my office within, bound in gold, that has the name of every DMP man that has ever served the crown. Do you wish for your own name to be added in due course?

RECRUIT. Oh — indeed and I do, sir. Most fervently.

THOMAS. I hope you will do well, son. These are troubled times, and men like yourself are sorely needed. I will be watching your progress — watching, you understand, in a fatherly way. Do your best.

RECRUIT. I will, sir. Thank you, sir!

THOMAS. *(Taking his hand.)* I was a young recruit myself once. I know what this means to you.

RECRUIT. The world, sir, it means the world.

THOMAS. Good man. I'll write to your father in Longford. Take this now as a token of our good faith. *(Handing him the spoon.)*

RECRUIT. Thank you, sir, thank you. *(The Recruit shadows away. Thomas kneels at the end of his bed and grips the metal tightly.)*

THOMAS. I must not speak to shadows. When you see the shadows, Thomas, you must not speak. Sleep in the afternoon, that's the ticket. How did I get myself into this pickle, is it age just? I know I did what Annie said I did, but was it really me, and not some old disreputable creature that isn't me? When it was over, I knew suddenly in the car coming here what had happened, but at the time, at the time, I knew nothing, or I knew something else. And it was the gap between the two things that caused me to cry out in the car, the pain of it, the pain of it, the fright of it, and no one in the world to look at me again in a manner that would suggest that Thomas Dunne is still human, still himself. Everything is as clear as a glass. I can remember how lovely Cissy was the day we married, and that smile she gave me when the priest was finished, how she looked up at me in front of all our people, her face shining, astonishing me. You don't expect to see love like that. And that's a long time ago. And I can remember, now, the last day with Annie, and how I was feeling that day, and I can see myself there in the kitchen, and I know how mad I was. And I am ashamed. I am ashamed. I am ashamed. *(After a while of breathing like a runner.)* Hail Mary, full of Grace, the Lord is with thee, blessed art Thou amongst women, and blessed is the fruit of Thy womb. *(He gets stuck, bangs his head with his right palm.)* — Jesus. Holy Mary, mother of. Holy Mary, mother of. I remember, I do remember. Hail Mary full of grace the Lord is with me blessed art Thou amongst women and blessed is the fruit of Thy womb Jesus holy Mary Mother of ... of ... of God! Of God! *(Climbs into bed.)* Robert Emmet. *(Pulls the sheet over his face.)* Robert Emmet. *(Spits the t's so the sheet blows up from his lips.)* Robert Emmet. *(After a moment.)* Sleep, sleep, that's the ticket. *(His son, Willie, neat and round, comes in and sits on the end of his bed and sings to him Shubert's "Ave Maria." At the end, Thomas looks over the sheet. Willie wears his army uniform.)* Hello, child. Are you warm?

WILLIE. It's cold in the mud, Father.

THOMAS. I know, child. I'm so sorry. *(Sunlight grows slowly over the scene, banishing Willie. The imagined stir and calling of the Castle below. Thomas is at ease suddenly. His middle daughter, Annie, in a light cotton dress of the early twenties, a bow in her spine, carries on a white shirt, which illumines like a lantern when she crosses the window light. There's an old music.)*

ANNIE. Now, Papa — there's the best-ironed shirt in Christendom.

THOMAS. Thank you, dear.

ANNIE. It took the best part of an hour to heat the hearth, to heat the iron. There's enough starch in the breast to bolster Jericho.

THOMAS. Thank you, dear.

ANNIE. If Dolly had ironed it, you'd look at it more intently.

THOMAS.   I am looking at it, Annie. Or I would, if it weren't so blinding white.

ANNIE.   And it isn't that white, Papa. And you've things on your mind today, I know. A black day.

THOMAS.   I expect it is.

ANNIE.   Why Collins of all people to give the Castle to? Couldn't they find a gentleman?

THOMAS.   He is the head of the new government, Annie.

ANNIE.   Government! We know what sort of men they are. Coming in here to the likes of you. Whose son gave his life for Ireland.

THOMAS.   *(Coming over to her, kindly.)* Will gave his life to save Europe, Annie, which isn't the same thing.

ANNIE.   I miss Willie, Papa. I miss him. We need him today.

THOMAS.   I blame myself. There was no need for him to go off, except, he hadn't the height to be a policeman. The army were glad to take him. I blame myself.

ANNIE.   Will was proud, Papa, proud to be in the Rifles. It was his life.

THOMAS.   It was the death of him. You cannot lose a son without blaming yourself. But that's all history now. Annie. *(Maud, his eldest, a very plain woman with black hair, dressed heavily for the bright day, carries on his dress uniform, struggling to balance the ceremonial sword.)* Let me help you.

MAUD.   It's all right, Papa, I'll plonk it on the bed.

THOMAS.   Where's Dolly?

MAUD.   Polishing the boots. I hate to see a woman spit. Lord, Lord, she's a spitter, when it's Papa's old shoes. And she was away out this morning, I know not why, all secretive.

ANNIE.   Away out this morning? She didn't touch her bed all night. Up at that dance at the Rotunda. She should be whipped.

MAUD.   And did you say she could go to that dance?

ANNIE.   I didn't say she could take all night to walk home.

THOMAS.   Thoughtful daughters you are, to be helping me so. How did you get the creases so firm?

MAUD.   I slept on them. In as much as I slept. I cannot sleep these times.

THOMAS. I could meet the emperor of the world with those creases.

ANNIE. You'll have to make do with Michael Collins.

MAUD. Oh, don't start that old story, Annie. We've had enough of it now, God knows.

ANNIE. I was only saying.

MAUD. Well, don't be only saying. Go and stir the teapot, can't you, and give over the politics.

ANNIE. I was only saying.

MAUD. You're only always only saying, and you have me stark wide-eyed in the bed all night, worrying and turning and fretting, and a great headache pounding away, because you can leave nothing alone, Annie, till you have us all miserable and mad with concern.

THOMAS. Now, girls, think of your mother. Would she want you to be talking like this?

MAUD. No, Papa, of course not. She would not.

ANNIE. Mam? What do you know about Mam, if I may ask?

MAUD. Don't I see her often when I sleep? Don't I see her blue polka-dot dress, yes, and her bending down to me and making me laugh?

ANNIE. That's only ould stuff Willie told us.

MAUD. Oh, Annie, Annie, I was four years old, you were only two!

THOMAS. Daughters, daughters — what a terrible thing to be arguing about!

ANNIE. Oh, a thing indeed.

MAUD. *(After a little.)* I'm sorry, Annie.

ANNIE. That's all right, girl. It's not your fault Collins is a criminal.

MAUD. I'll be dead, that's it! I'll be dead by day's end. I can't take everything in! My head's bursting with Papa and Michael Collins and I don't know what.... *(Dolly, holding out the polished boots carefully from her dress, starts across to Thomas, smiling. Thomas' face lights like a lamp.)*

THOMAS. Oh, Dolly, Dolly, Dolly! *(Before she reaches him, an intrusion of darkness, the scattering of his daughters. Thomas roars, with pain and confusion. He lifts his arms and roars. He beats the bed. He hits the table. He roars. Smith unlocks the door and hurries in, brandishing a pacifier. It looks like a baton.)*

SMITH.   What the hell is all the shouting? You have the pauper lunatics in a swelter! Crying and banging their heads, and laughing like fairground mechanicals, and spitting, and cutting themselves with items. *(Looking back out.)* Mrs. O'Dea, Mrs. O'Dea — try and sort those screamers!

MRS. O'DEA.   *(Off.)* I will, I will!

SMITH.   Even the long ward of old dames with their dead brains, have some of them opened their eyes and are weeping to be woken, with your bloody shouting. Do you want to go in with them, old man? After I beat you!

THOMAS.   *(Hurrying back into his bed.)* I only shouted the one time. It must have been the moon woke them. *(Drawing the sheet high.)* My daughter Annie gives you the shillings for the room, Black Jim.

SMITH.   She can give all the shillings she likes. She won't know where we throw you.

THOMAS.   Don't put Thomas with the poor dribblers. I've seen them. I've seen that terrible long ward of women, belonging to no one at all, no one to pay shillings for them. Don't put me there.

SMITH.   Then show me silence. *(Striking the end of the bed.)*

THOMAS.   Don't strike there. My son sits there.

SMITH.   You are a violent, stupid man, Mr. Dunne, and I want silence out of you!

THOMAS.   *(A finger to his lips.)* Silence. *(Smith goes, banging the door, locking it harshly. Pulling up the sheet.)* Robert Emmet. *(Annie has slipped over to his bed.)*

ANNIE.   Papa.

THOMAS.   *(Looking out again.)* I must be silent, child.

ANNIE.   Papa, please will you tell me.

THOMAS.   What, child?

ANNIE.   Why is my back bowed, Papa?

THOMAS.   Why, child, because of your polio.

ANNIE.   Why, Papa?

THOMAS.   I don't know, Annie. Because it afflicts some and

leaves others clear. I don't know.

ANNIE. Will I ever have a husband, Papa?

THOMAS. I do hope so.

ANNIE. I think a woman with such a back will not find a husband.

THOMAS. She might.

ANNIE. I see the prams going by in Stephen's Green, glistening big prams, and I look in when the nannies are polite, and I look in, and I see the babies, with their round faces, and their smells of milk and clean linen, and their heat and Papa—

THOMAS. Yes, child?

ANNIE. They all look like my babies. *(Annie goes, Thomas looks after her, then covers his face again. A country music. He sleeps, he sleeps. The moon, the emblem of lunacy, appears overhead, pauses there faintly, fades again. It is a very delicate, strange sleep. The calling of a cock distantly, birdsong, the cock louder. An arm of sunlight creeps into the room and across Thomas' covered face. His hand creeps out and his fingers wave in the light. He pulls down the sheet and the noises cease. He listens. Imitates the cock softly.)*

THOMAS. The cock crows in the morning yard, banishing all night fears. No person, that has not woken to the crowing of a familiar cock, can know how tender that cry is evermore, stirring the child out into the fresh fingers of sunlight, into the ever-widening armfuls of sunlight. How stray the child looks in the yard, bare feet on the old pack stones in the clay, all his people have come out in their own vanished times, as small as him, surrounded by the quiet byres just wakening now, the noses of the calves wet in the closed dark, the sitting hens in the coop anxious to be released, out away from the night fear of foxes, so they may lay their eggs beyond finding in the hayshed and the hawthorn bushes. Only the boy knows their terrible tricks. He inserts an arm into the known places and feels the warm eggs, smells them happily in his brown palms, and searches out the newest places of the hens in the deepest bowers of the straw. He carries them back in to his Ma Ma, folded in his gansey, with the glow of pride about him as big as the sun. Then he goes back out into the yard while the eggs are boiling, or put aside carefully for the cake, and tries to read

21

the story of the day in the huge pages of the clouds. And he sees the milking cow driven up on to the top field where the summer grass is rich and moist, and how well he knows the wild garden there of meadowsweet, where the dragonfly is hard as pencil. And the boy's Ma Ma is calling him, and he goes, and there is no greater morning, no morning in his life of greater importance. *(Smith enters with a newspaper. He fetches out Thomas' pot. It's empty.)*

SMITH.   I hope you're not blocking up like some of the old fellows.

THOMAS.   A deserted house needs no gutter. Is that my newspaper?

SMITH.   It is. *(Throws it to him. Thomas opens it.)* Can you not order a decent newspaper?

THOMAS.   *Irish Times* suits me.

SMITH.   It's all fools on horseback.

THOMAS.   Not so much. I'm trying to keep up on the activities, if I may call them that, of a certain Hinky Dink Kenna, who runs the first ward in Chicago. I tell you, you'd have to call him a criminal here. Himself and Bath-house John Coughlan. Villains. If they had never left Ireland, I'd have had to lock them up in Mountjoy. But you can do what you like in America, or so it seems.

SMITH.   Is that right? And what do they get up to, those two?

THOMAS.   Oh, they're in the liquor trade, you might say. It makes powerful reading. *(Mrs. O'Dea comes in with big flaps of black cloth — Thomas' suit in its unsewn parts.)*

SMITH.   He hasn't washed himself.

MRS. O'DEA.   Didn't you wash him yesterday? Do you want to rub him out? Come on up, Mr. Dunne, and let me pin these to you for a look at it.

SMITH.   Can't you see he's reading.

THOMAS.   *(Getting out of bed.)* Oh, I've time for reading. In my retirement. *(He stands for the fitting. Mrs. O'Dea begins to pin the sections of the suit to his long johns.)*

MRS. O'DEA.   You're the cleanest man in Baltinglass. *(Thomas seems agitated, looking down at the sections.)* What's the matter, Mr. Dunne?

THOMAS. That's just the old black stuff.

MRS. O'DEA. And what if it is?

THOMAS. *(So Smith won't hear.)* Didn't we discuss yellow?

MRS. O'DEA. Yellow thread, Mr. Dunne. I can only stitch the sections together with yellow. The trustees buy us in the black cloth from Antrim.

THOMAS. But it's fierce, foul stuff, isn't it?

SMITH. I'll leave you to it, Mrs. O'Dea. I'll be over in the Monkey Ward, sluicing them out, if you need me. Be good, Mr. Dunne. *(Goes.)*

MRS. O'DEA. *(Taking a bobbin from her apron.)* Look it, isn't that the bee's knees? That's from my own sewing box, that Mr. O'Dea gave me in the old days. I can't do fairer than that.

THOMAS. Oh, it's very sunny.

MRS. O'DEA. Now. *(Pinning again.)* It'll do beautifully. Can't your daughter bring you in clothes, if you don't like mine?

THOMAS. I wouldn't go bothering her. All my daughters are good, considerate women. We looked after each other, in that fled time, when their mother was dead.

MRS. O'DEA. I'm sorry, Mr. Dunne. And how did she die?

THOMAS. They never failed their father, their Papa, in that fled time. You should have seen them when they were little. Three little terrors going round with the knicks to their knees.

MRS. O'DEA. *(Pricking him by mistake.)* Oh, sorry. And where are your other daughters, Mr. Dunne, these days?

THOMAS. We stood under the hawthorn, while the bees broke their hearts at the bell-flowers, because the fringes of darkness had closed them.

MRS. O'DEA. Who did, Mr. Dunne?

THOMAS. My wife Cissy and myself. Cecilia. In courting days. Old courting days.

MRS. O'DEA. And what did she die of, did you say? *(Pricking.)*

THOMAS. Nothing at all. Her farm was Lathaleer, her father's farm. The most beautiful piece of land. He was woodsman and keeper at Humewood, but he was a most dexterous farmer. The Cullens of Lathaleer. What a match she was for me! A strong, straight-backed, sensible person that loved old steps and tunes. She'd rather learn a new step than boil turnips, old Cullen said to me — but it wasn't so. What does a father know? King Edward himself praised her hair, when we were presented in nineteen-three. A thorough mole-black devious hair she had.

MRS. O'DEA.   I'm sure. And didn't you do well by her, rising so high, and everything?

THOMAS.   Our happiest days were when I was only an inspector in Dalkey village. We lived there in a house called Polly Villa. There was precious little villainy in Dalkey. Three girls she bore there, three girls. And the boy already, before we came.

MRS. O'DEA.   You have a son too? You have a lot.

THOMAS.   No. No, he didn't come back from France that time. He wrote me a lovely letter.

MRS. O'DEA.   *(After a little.)* And King Edward praised your wife's hair. Fancy.

THOMAS.   Aye — All the ladies loved him. Of course, he was old in that time. But a true king.

MRS. O'DEA.   *(Finished with the fitting, unpinning him again.)* What would you say about King De Valera?

THOMAS.   I would say very little about him, in that I wouldn't know much to say. Of course, I see a bit about him in the papers.

MRS. O'DEA.   As much a foreigner as the King of England ever was, Mr. O'Dea used to say, when he was overground. Mr. O'Dea was a pundit, I'm afraid.

THOMAS.   He wants to buy the Irish ports back from Mr. Churchill. I think that's a great pity. A man that loves his King might still have gone to live in Crosshaven or Cobh, and called himself loyal and true. But soon there'll be nowhere in Ireland where such hearts may rest.

MRS. O'DEA.   You're as well to keep up with the news, Mr. Dunne.

THOMAS.   I had an admiration for the other man though, the general that was shot, I forget his name.

MRS. O'DEA.   *(Ready to go.)* Who was that?

THOMAS.   I forget. I remember the shock of sorrow when he was killed. I remember Annie and me crying in the old parlour of our quarters in the Castle. A curiosity. I met him, you see, the one time. He was very courteous and praised Wicklow and said a few things to me that rather eased my heart, at the time. But they shot him.

MRS. O'DEA. *(Going.)* They shot a lot of people. Was it Collins?

THOMAS. I don't know, I forget. I remember the sorrow but not the name. Maybe that was the name.

MRS. O'DEA. I may have left a few pins in you, Mr. Dunne, so don't go dancing about unduly.

THOMAS. Dancing? I never danced in my life. I was a tree at a dance. *(Mrs. O'Dea goes off. Thomas discovers a pin and holds it up.)* Where are your other daughters, Mr. Dunne, these days? The barracks of Ireland filled with new faces. And all the proud regiments gone, the Dublin Rifles and the Dublin Fusiliers. All the lovely uniforms. All the long traditions, broken up and flung out, like so many morning egg on to the dung heap. Where are your other daughters, Mr. Dunne, these days? Dolly of the hats. Annie told me the name of the place. Somewhere in America. What was the name? *(The light of their parlour in the Castle. Annie comes on with a big bundle of socks to sort. She sits on the three-legged stool. The socks are all the same. She looks in the socks for holes by thrusting her right hand into each of them, sorts the good from the bad.)*

ANNIE. There's a terrible queer sort of a quietness settled over this Castle. How Papa expects to hang on here now till September. The city will be rubble, rubble by September. *(Maud follows on looking pale and alarmed.)*

MAUD. Have you seen that Dolly?

ANNIE. No.

MAUD. I can't keep a hoult on her at all these days.

ANNIE. She'll be down the town, as usual.

MAUD. How can she go shopping in times like these?

ANNIE. What's civil unrest to Dolly and her shopping?

MAUD. *(Feeling the back of her head.)* Oh, dear.

ANNIE. What is it, Maud?

MAUD. Nothing, nothing at all.

ANNIE. Maud, what is it now?

25

MAUD.   I have an ache here, Annie, at the base of the skull, do you think it might be something deadly?

ANNIE.   I never knew a one to worry like you do, girl.

MAUD.   Do you want to feel it? Is there a lump?

ANNIE.   Don't come near me with your head! It's nothing. It's called a headache. Any normal person would accept that it's a headache. Girl, sometimes I don't wonder if you mightn't be seriously astray in your wits, girl.

MAUD.   Oh, don't say that, Annie.

ANNIE.   Am I not allowed sort the darning in peace? *(Dolly comes in to them, wearing a neat outfit. She looks subdued.)* What's happened you, Dolly?

MAUD.   I was all over the yards looking for you, Dolly, where on earth do you get to, these days?

DOLLY.   I was down at the North Wall with the Galligan sisters.

MAUD.   At the North Wall?

ANNIE.   What were you doing there, Dolly?

DOLLY.   Mary Galligan was going out with one of the Tommies, and he and his troop were heading off home today, so we went down to see them off.

ANNIE.   *(Sorting away.)* Well, well, I don't know, Dolly, if you aren't the biggest fool in Christendom.

DOLLY.   No, I'm no fool. They were nice lads. There was a good crowd down there, and the Tommies were in high spirits, singing and so on. It was very joyful.

MAUD.   You've to keep your skirts long these times, Dolly. You're not to be seen waving to soldiers.

DOLLY.   They're going from Ireland and they'll never be back, why shouldn't we say goodbye? Do you know every barracks in Ireland has lost its officers and men? Regiments that protected us in the war, who went out and left thousands behind in France. Willie's own regiment is to be disbanded, and that's almost entirely Dublin lads.

ANNIE.   Dolly, why are you so surprised? Haven't we known for the last six months that Ireland is to be destroyed? I don't know why it's such news to you. Haven't you listened? Haven't you seen your father's face? Haven't you felt for him, Dolly?

DOLLY. It's different when you see it.

ANNIE. You're a fool, Dolly.

DOLLY. I'm no fool. *(Annie picks up in one hand the good socks and in the other the ones needing mending — they look like two woolly hands themselves.)* And I'll tell you. Coming home in the tram, up the docks road, Mary Galligan was crying, and we were talking kindly to her, and trying to comfort her, and I don't know what we said exactly, but this woman, a middle-aged woman, quite well-to-do, she rises up and stands beside us like a long streak of misery, staring at us. And she struck Mary Galligan on the cheek, so as she left the marks of her hand there. And she would have attacked me too, but that the conductor came down and spoke to the woman. And she said we were Jezebels and should have our heads shaved and be whipped, for following the Tommies. And the conductor looked at her, and hadn't he served in France himself, as one of the Volunteers, oh, it was painful, the way she looked back at him, as if he were a viper, or a traitor. The depth of foolishness in her. A man that had risked himself, like Willie, but that had reached home at last. *(Dolly crying. Annie gets up and puts her arms around her, still holding the socks.)*

ANNIE. Things will sort themselves out, Dolly dear.

DOLLY. If she had shot us it wouldn't have been so bad.

ANNIE. Things will sort themselves out. *(Maud feeling the back of her head again, confused.)* We'll put on our aprons and get the tea. We'll go on ourselves as if we were living in paradise. *(The three go out.)*

THOMAS. Their father's face. Their father's face. *(He puts his hands over his face. Matt, a youngish man in a hat, his shirt sleeves held by metal circlets, sets up his easel. Sunlight gathers about him, clearing the sense of Thomas' room. Rooks. A suggestion of meadow grass. Matt holds a square of cut-out cardboard to the view, deciding on a composition. He wipes at his face.)*

MATT. Midges! The artist's bane! *(Thomas approaches him, a little wildly.)*

THOMAS. Patrick O'Brien, Patrick O'Brien, wherever did you bury my suit, man dear? They are tormenting me with dark cloth, and I hope you will give it back to me, despite your great prowess and fame, as a bulleter.

MATT.   It isn't who you think, Thomas. It is Matt Kirwin that married your daughter Maud.

THOMAS.   *(Astonished.)* Oh — is it? *(After a moment.)* You have a strong look of Patrick about you. Except I see now, you are not on all fours, as I would expect. Are you a hero too?

MATT.   *(Kindly.)* How are you getting on, Thomas?

THOMAS.   How does it come that you are here in the walking meadow? I only ask, as I am used to seeing people hither and thither and yon. *(Feeling his arms for solidity.)* Have you lost your wits also?

MATT.   Maybe so, but I have brought Annie over in the Ford. We're over there in Kiltegan for a week or two with the little boys. I thought I might capture a water-colour while I waited.

THOMAS.   You might, like a man might capture a butterfly. You haven't started your capturing.

MATT.   In a minute, when I decide the view I want. The painting itself will only take a moment.

THOMAS.   They're all choice views. Where's Maud then?

MATT.   She stayed in Dublin this time.

THOMAS.   It isn't the melancholy?

MATT.   I don't know what it is. She has certainly kept to her bed of recent months. Has she been right since the second boy came? I don't know.

THOMAS.   Her mother was always very jolly. I don't know where she gets it from.

MATT.   The sea air of Howth will cure all that, in time, the sea air, the quieter nature of life there in Howth, and the boys. She does love to see the boys, and they are most dignified and splendid boys.

THOMAS.   You say? *(Warmly.)* Well, Matt, *(Taking Matt's hand.)* how are you? *(Oddly.)* How do you do?

MATT.   We're going along fine. I'm teaching in the technical school in Irishtown — for my sins. And painting for myself when I can. I have done a great deal of work on the Great South Wall, in my lunchtimes. The Poolbeg Lighthouse? But we couldn't get by at all without Annie. She keeps everything going.

THOMAS.   Yes, yes, she told me you had one of your drawings printed up in a book, didn't you, yes, of the Bailey Lighthouse I think she said. You will be a great expert soon on lighthouses.

MATT.   *(Pleased.)* It was little enough.

THOMAS.   Ah, Matthew, it is good to see you. You're looking so well. I forget, you know, I forget how much I like you. And the boys, the two grand boys, will I see them today? Are they in the Ford?

MATT.   No, Thomas. They're so little still, and this is such a strange spot, for children, and, you know, they were a bit upset the last time. The elder boy has read his *Oliver Twist* and you were all mixed up in his mind with Fagin. Do you remember, at the end of the book, when the child is brought in to see Fagin before Fagin is hanged?

THOMAS.   Hanged? No.

MATT.   Maud was worried that....

THOMAS.   Certainly, certainly. You must excuse my long johns. I lost my suit only recently. As a matter of fact, it must be buried around here somewhere. Well, no matter, they'll make me another, and then maybe you will bring my grandsons again to see me? Or you could fetch me over to Kiltegan in the Ford if they were afraid of this place. I'd be very quiet for you in the Ford.

MATT.   Of course, Thomas.

THOMAS.   I know I look a sight. And that won't do for such fine boys. I only saw them those few times, but, I think it is the smell of children that gets in upon you. You long for it then. And the roundness of them, and the love they show you. It could be anywhere about here, my suit. But I'm having a touch of gold put into the new one — well, yellow, anyhow.

MATT.   You'll find Annie in your room if you go up, I'll be bound. She thought you were inside, you know.

THOMAS.   Yellow thread, you know?

MATT.   All right.

THOMAS.   Matt, I don't like to ask Annie, to bother her, but do you think there's any great likelihood of my getting away from here at all in the coming times?

29

MATT.   I don't know rightly, Thomas.

THOMAS.   Of course, of course. It is quite a pleasant station. You see all the country air we have. Not like the city. The city would ruin a man's health. Though it has its beauties. Do you know, I used at one time to be a policeman? Do you know I used at one time be Chief Superintendent of B Division? With responsibility for the Castle herself? It was I cleared all the vermin out of Yorke Street, that time, the fancy men from the Curragh and all their girls — it *was* me, wasn't it, Matt? I held that post? You must bring the boys to Kiltegan as often as you can.

MATT.   Well, we do, Thomas. You have a fine vista here, look. *(Having him look into the cardboard framer.)* You do, what with those oaks, and the field of wheat beyond.

THOMAS.   *(Peering, after a moment.)* It's only grass just.

MATT.   Oh, is it grass?

THOMAS.   Paint away, Matthew.

MATT.   Thank you. *(The light of Thomas' room again finds Annie, more spinsterish now, strong, bony, simply dressed, with her handbag and a brown paper bag. She looks anxious. Thomas goes to her with a great smile, raising his arms.)*

THOMAS.   *(Searching in his mind for her name.)* Dolly — Maud — Annie!

ANNIE.   Papa.

THOMAS.   *(His arms collapsing slowly.)* What has happened to you, Annie? You look very different to how you were just this morning.

ANNIE.   What happened to your clothes, Papa?

THOMAS.   I don't know, Dolly.

ANNIE.   Annie, it is.

THOMAS.   Annie. I don't know. I think I heard there was a bit of thievery going on, but I don't think there's any truth in it. Nothing for the magistrate. I'll deal with it. You know Mr. Collins is to take over the Castle in January. I'll need all my clothes done over like new.

ANNIE.   No, Papa. That was all years ago. In bygone times. You are in Baltinglass County Home, Papa.

THOMAS.   I know. And I tell myself, so I won't forget. I had

30

it written down somewhere, but I lost the bit of paper. What is it about the old head? Give me the name of any street in Dublin and I'll name every lane, alleyway, road, terrace and street around it. I could knit you the whole thing with names, and if you forgot a few places, and found a hole there in your memory, I could darn it for you. I am in effect a sort of Dublin Street Directory. But when it comes to the brass tacks of things, everyday matters, as, for instance, where in the name of God I am, well, daughter dear, I'm not so quick then. But look, girl, what Annie gave me. *(Going to his mattress and fetching a book out.)* A wonderful strange story about a boy on the Mississippi. And his friend. They are lost in a cave together, the two boys, and the poor bit of a greasy candle they have is burning lower and lower, and the demons of the dark are surely approaching … I feel I know that cave. Do you see, Dolly? I can see it when I put my hands over my face. Like this. Yes, there she is, the mighty Mississippi, going along like Godly pewter. And those poor boys, Huckleberry and Tom, and the yellow walls of the cave, and the big drips of water. Oh, Dolly, and the old granite bathing place at Vico Rock. And there's the terrible suck-up of water when Davy Barnes the newspaper vendor takes his dive, the fattest man in Ireland, and there's Annie, all decked out in her first communion regalia like a princess, oh, mercy, and there's the moon over a bay that reputable people have compared to Naples — Sorrento, Vico, beautiful Italian names living the life of Reilly in old Killiney and Dalkey. On a summer's night, you were born, Dolly, deep in the fresh dark, just when the need for candles failed. Oh, Dolly.

ANNIE.   *(Trying to calm him.)* I gave you the book about the Mississippi, Papa. It's a book you loved in your youth, so you always said.

THOMAS.   *(Gripping her arm a bit roughly.)* Where is Maud, where is she, that she doesn't come in to me?

ANNIE.   She's taken refuge, taken refuge you might say, in her own difficulties.

THOMAS.   Is that right? And Dolly, where is Dolly?

ANNIE.   Gone out into the wide world, Papa. Would you blame her?

THOMAS. Blame her? *(Formal again.)* How do you do? How is Maud? How are the boys? No, no, I know all that. Don't tell me. I won't waste your time, never you fear. How are you? That's the important thing to establish. That's how people go on among themselves, family people. Is there any word from Dolly in America? Annie, Annie, where is she in America?

ANNIE. Ohio, Papa.

THOMAS. Ohio, Ohio! That's the place. Ah, I was tormented trying to think of the word. Ohio. Dolly in Ohio. I must write it down. Do you have a dragonfly — a pencil?

ANNIE. No, Papa, I don't. This room is so bare and dark, for all the shillings I give them. I hope they give you your paper. It's all I can manage, Papa, out of your pension. It is a very miserly pension. Matt makes up the rest of it for us. And he has a pittance.

THOMAS. Don't I have a beautiful pension for my forty-five years of service?

ANNIE. No, Papa, you don't.

THOMAS. I think I should have.

ANNIE. Look, Papa, what I brought for you. *(She pulls a bunch of heather from the bag.)*

THOMAS. Oh, Lord, Lord. *(Smelling it in his hands tenderly.)* From the hills above Kiltegan. How the heat of the day makes the heather raise its smell to the grateful native. The peace, the deep peace in the evening as we stared, you and me, into the last lingering flames running across the ashen turf, and the ghostly tiredness in us after slaving about the place all day.

ANNIE. When was that, Papa?

THOMAS. Those three years in Kiltegan, Annie, when you and me were left to amuse ourselves as we could, Annie. You remember?

ANNIE. I do, Papa, I remember the three years well enough. With you sinking lower and lower in your chair beside that fire, and muttering about this and that, and the way you had been abandoned, you wouldn't treat a dog like that, you said, muttering, muttering, till I was driven mad. And all the work of the dairy and the byre and the hens to do. It was like living with Hannibal in Abyssinia, when Hannibal was a leader no more.

32

THOMAS. Who? Where? But didn't the Cullens of Lathaleer come visiting like royalty in their high trap, and the Dunnes of Feddin, and the Cullens of Kelsha?

ANNIE. No, Papa, they did not, not after you drove them away with insult and passing remarks.

THOMAS. I never did. We lived there like, like....

ANNIE. Like, like the dead, Papa.

THOMAS. *(Angry.)* All right. So there were demons in the high wood, and the screams of the lost from the byres, and the foul eggs in the rotting hay, and every pitchfork in the barn was sharp, glinting sharp, for you to thrust into my breast.

ANNIE. Papa, Papa, calm and ease, calm and ease.

THOMAS. Oh, fearsome, fearsome, fearsome. Can I see my grandsons?

ANNIE. *(Holding on to her father.)* Papa, Papa. Your grandsons are afraid of you.

THOMAS. Afraid? Filthy, filthy.

ANNIE. Papa, Papa. How many miles to Babylon?

THOMAS. *(Smiling.)* Babylon.

ANNIE. Three score and ten. Remember, Papa, remember?

THOMAS. Will I be there by candlelight?

ANNIE. Sure, and back again.

THOMAS. Candlelight. Oh, yes, yes. *(Weeping.)* Yes. *(Smiling.)* Yes.

ANNIE. How many times in that last year in Kiltegan did I have to sing you the songs to calm your fears?

THOMAS. Was it so many?

ANNIE. Many, many, many. Three score and ten, Papa.

THOMAS. *(After a long breath.)* My father was the steward of Humewood, and I was the steward of Christendom. Look at me.

ANNIE. Papa, we've all to grow old.

THOMAS. *(Patting her back with his right hand, like a child.)* Oh, yes. Oh, yes. *(Annie goes quietly. Thomas sits on the stool slowly. The door ajar.)* Candlelight. *(After a little.)* A bit of starch for a new shirt, a bit of spit for my shoes, I could set out for Kiltegan as an ordinary man and see those shining boys. *(After a little.)* No. *(After a little.)* And take them up and smell their hair and kiss their noses and make them do that laughter they have in them. *(After a little.)* No. *(After a little.)* Dear Lord, put the recruits back in their barracks in Fitzgibbon Street, put the stout hearts back into Christendom's Castle, and troop the colours once more for Princess and Prince, for Queen and for King, for Chief Secretary and Lord Lieutenant, for Viceroy and Commander-in-Chief. *(After a little.)* But you cannot. *(After a little.)* Put the song back in the mouth of the beggar, the tune back in the penny whistle, the rat-tat-tat of the tattoo back in the parade ground, stirring up our hearts. *(After a little.)* But you cannot. *(After a little.)* — Gone. The hearth of Kiltegan. How many miles to Kiltegan, Nineveh and Babylon? The sun amiable in the yard and the moon in the oaks after darkness. The rabbit-man stepping out of the woods at dusk with a stick of dangling snags and a dark greeting. — Gone. *(After a little, quietly.)* Candlelight. I walked out through the grounds of Loreto College as far as the sea. The midwife had bade me go. I was a man of fifty. Rhododendrons. All night she had strained in the bed, she was like a person pinned by a fallen rock, waving her arms and legs and groaning, and shouting. Her shouts escaped from Polly Villa and ran up the road to the station and down the road to the village in darkness. I was becoming distressed myself, so the midwife bade me go. Willie, Maud and Annie had been difficult for her too, because she was small, small and thin and hardworking. Cullen's daughter. And she was like a sort of dancer in the bed, but stuck in the dance. King Edward himself praised her hair, it was mole-black, though there are no moles in Ireland. Out at sea, the lighthouse was hard at work too, warning the mail-packet and the night fishermen. I thought of all the nuns asleep up in the college, asleep in their quiet rooms, the sea asleep herself at the foot of the cliff. And I thought, I would do anything for that woman of mine behind me in the house, where we had done all our talking and laughing and our quarrelling. But my mind was in a peculiar state. I thought of all the Sunday roasts she had made, all piled up somewhere in eternity, a measure of her expertise. And I thought of how much her daughters and her son loved her, and depended on her for every sort of information, and how stupid and silent I was with my son. How she made the world possible and hopeful for him and the two girls. *(Sits on bed.)* I started to tremble, it was a moment in your life when daily things pass away from you, when all your concerns seem to vanish, and you are allowed by God a little space of clarity and grace. When you see that God himself is in your wife and in your children, and they hold in trust for you your own measure of goodness. And in the manner of your treatment of them lies your own salvation. I went back to the house with a lighter heart, a simpler man than the one who had set out. And the house was quiet. It was as if it were itself asleep, the very bricks, living and asleep with a quiet heartbeat. *(Holding the pillow.)* Suddenly I was terribly afeared that my new child was dead, I don't know why. You expect its cries, you long for its cries. I pushed open my front door and hurried down into the back room. The midwife was over by the window, with a little bundle. And Cissy was lying quiet, still, at ease. The midwife came over immediately and placed her bundle in my arms. It was like holding a three-pound bag of loose corn. *(The pillow.)* And there was a little face in the midst of the linen, a little wrinkled face, with red skin, and two big round eyes seeming to look up at me. I pledged all my heart and life to that face, all my blood and strength to that face, all the usefulness of my days to that face. And that was Dolly. And that was just as the need for candlelight fails, and the early riser needs no candle for his task. *(Music. Dark after a few moments.)*

ACT TWO

Thomas' room as before. Maud holding his sword in readiness. Annie near. Dolly looking at Thomas with the polished shoes just on. He wears his dress uniform, the helmet as yet on the table.

THOMAS. Oh, Dolly, Dolly, Dolly.

DOLLY. Will they do, Papa?

THOMAS. They're beautiful shoes now.

DOLLY. This whole day reminds me of when I was twelve, and there were snipers on the roofs above the music-hall, and me and Annie and Maud would be crawling along the sandbags outside the gates, trying to get in home from the shops. And laughing. And the soldiers at the gates laughing too.

ANNIE. That poor lieutenant didn't laugh when they put a bullet in his head.

MAUD. And you were only ten then, Miss Dolly, and as wild as a tenement cat.

DOLLY. Will it be like that today?

THOMAS. No, sweet, that's all done with now. This is an act of peace.

ANNIE. My foot.

THOMAS. *(Putting an arm about Dolly.)* Mr. Collins and a small staff will come in, and we'll all meet like gentlemen.

ANNIE. Ha.

THOMAS. And he will take command of the place, in effect. Don't you worry, Dolly, don't you worry.

DOLLY. And what time is the meeting, Papa?

THOMAS. Shortly. The chief secretary wanted to meet at six but Collins sent in a note to say he wasn't a blackbird.

ANNIE. Blackguard more like.

DOLLY. You are sure no one will try to shoot you?

THOMAS. Why would they want to shoot me?

ANNIE. They would hardly have offered Papa a position in

their new police force if they wanted to shoot him.

DOLLY. Did they, Papa? Oh, and will you take up that offer, Papa? It would be exciting.

THOMAS. We'll be Wicklow people again by year's end. Look at your father, Dolly. I am sixty-six years old! I am too old for new things. Indeed, I wish I were a younger man again, and I could kiss your noses, like when you were babies, and make you scream with delight.

MAUD. Papa! Come along, Papa, and we'll get your sword on you. *(Maud and Annie attach the sword to its belt.)*

THOMAS. A man with three such daughters, three beautiful daughters, will never be entirely worthless. This January morning is the start of peace, and we may enjoy that peace till September, and then be gone — gone like shadows of an old dispensation.

DOLLY. A girl of eighteen is never a shadow, Papa.

THOMAS. Today is — what do you call it — symbolical. *(Maud doing the last buttons on the jacket.)* Like those banners in the Chapel Royal for every lord lieutenant that has ruled Ireland. It's a mighty symbolical sort of a day, after all these dark years. I'll be worn out. I'll be practising now. *(Taking Dolly's hand.)* Good man, Joe, good man, Harry — that's the constables, because they're young too, Dolly, and will be greatly affected. Oh, big country hands, with rural grips! I'll have crushed fingers, like a visiting king.

ANNIE. And well, Papa, you are a king, more than some of those other scallywags.

THOMAS. That is the whole crux of the matter. I am not a king. I am the servant of a king. I am only one of the stewards of his Irish city.

ANNIE. Collins is no king either, begging your pardon. With a tally of carnage, intrigue and disloyalty that would shame a tinker. And that King, for all his moustaches and skill on horseback, has betrayed us.

MAUD. Annie, Annie, be quiet while Papa goes out. It isn't Papa's fault.

THOMAS. I served that King, Annie, and that will suffice me. I hope I guarded his possession well, and helped the people

37

through a terrible time. And now that story is over and I am over with it, and content. I don't grieve.

MAUD.   Of course you don't. Won't we have the great days soon in Kiltegan?

THOMAS.   But won't Dolly miss the fashions and the shops and the to-do of the town?

ANNIE.   *(Before Dolly can answer.)* I'll miss nothing. If they want to destroy everything, let them do so without us. It will be whins and waste everywhere, with bits of stones sticking up that were once Parliament, Castle and Cathedral. And people going round like scarecrows and worse. And Cuckoo Lane and Red Cow Lane and all those places just gaps with rubbish in them.

MAUD.   Annie, you're giving me a powerful headache.

ANNIE.   The like of Collins and his murdering men won't hold this place together. They haven't the grace or the style for it. So you needn't mourn your shops and hats and haircuts, Dolly Dunne — they won't be there.

THOMAS.   Will I tell Mr. Collins you said so, Annie?

MAUD.   You'll miss the show if you don't go now, Papa. You don't want to be running over the square to them and sweating in your finery.

THOMAS.   Am I shipshape?

MAUD.   Shipshape as a ship.

DOLLY.   Wait, don't let the King go! *(Hurrying out for something.)*

THOMAS.   Where's she off to now?

ANNIE.   Who can say where Dolly goes.

MAUD.   Poor Dolly — I do feel sorry for her.

ANNIE.   Why for Dolly? Feel sorry for yourself, woman.

DOLLY.   *(Coming back with a buttonhole.)* I got this for you last night, Papa.

ANNIE.   On that dangerous trek back from the dance at the Rotunda....

DOLLY.   *(Looking at Annie.)* Fresh up from the country.

ANNIE.   I hope you can wear a buttonhole today? It seems frivolous.

THOMAS.   Put it in for me, Dolly. A white rose! Now I'm ready for them.

DOLLY. *(Catching sight of the heather on the table.)* Oh, but, Papa, you'd flowers already — maybe you meant to wear a bit of this?

ANNIE. It isn't there at all yet. Just mere hints of flowers. That heather was born in the snow.

MAUD. *(Smelling it.)* That heather was born in the snow, right enough, Annie.

ANNIE. *(Drawn to the heather, as are Thomas and Dolly.)* It came up on the Wicklow train. Sometimes you find you need a hint of home.

DOLLY. Born in the snow, like a lamb.

THOMAS. That's from the hill beside the sloping field. I know that colour. *(Smelling, all of them smelling.)* It smells like God's breath, it does.

MAUD. We won't mind going home to such riches.

THOMAS. It is the very honeyed lord of a smell, so it is. *(Thomas goes out the door happily. The daughters scatter. Then the noise of a ruckus in the corridor.)*

SMITH. *(Off.)* Where are you wandering to? *(After a little.)* Where are you heading, old man?

THOMAS. *(Off.)* What are you saying to me, constable? — Get back from me!

SMITH. *(Off.)* Mrs. O'Dea, Mrs. O'Dea! Lie in there against the wall, you scarecrow, you. Mrs. O'Dea! Come up, come up!

MRS. O'DEA. *(Off.)* Oh, I'm hurrying, I'm hurrying.... *(Mrs. O'Dea steps into the room.)*

THOMAS. *(Off.)* But I have to go and meet Collins!

SMITH. *(Off.)* Collins is stone dead. *(Thomas, in his long johns again, propelled in by Smith.)*

THOMAS. Where are you putting me? This isn't our quarters!

SMITH. Who was it left his door open? He might have gone raving up the main street of Baltinglass.

MRS. O'DEA. I don't know. It must have been his daughter.

THOMAS. What have you done with my daughters? *(Pushing Smith.)* Get back from me, you blackguard. By Christ, assaulting a policeman. That's the Joy for you, you scoundrel.

SMITH. *(Drawing out the pacifier.)* Right, boy, I did warn you. Now you'll get it. *(Raising the implement.)* Mrs. O'Dea, fetch the jacket off the hook in the corridor. *(Mrs. O'Dea goes out.)* You'll see the suit she has for you now, Thomas Dunne.

THOMAS. You'll see the suit, Tomassy Tom. You'll see the suit. *(Thomas escapes from him, leaps the bed like a youth.)*

SMITH. Jesus of Nazareth. *(Smith goes after him, Thomas ducks around to the stool, Mrs. O'Dea brings in the strait-jacket.)*

THOMAS. Nicks, nicks.

SMITH. He's claiming nicks off the three-legged stool. *(Smith strides to Thomas and strikes him with the pacifier, expertly enough.)* Why couldn't I go with my brother flensing whales?

THOMAS. *(Wriggling.)* You think I haven't had worse? See this thumb? See the purple scar there? My own Da Da did that, with a sheath knife. What do you think of that? *(Smith struggles to place the jacket on him.)* Do you want to see my back? I've a mark there was done with a cooper's band, and on a Sunday too. But he loved me.

MRS. O'DEA. Lie up on your bed, Mr. Dunne. *(To Smith.)* He'll be worn out in a minute. I have your suit ready, Mr. Dunne, will I bring it up to you? He'll be good now, Mr. Smith.

THOMAS. *(Lying on the bed awkwardly, bound.)* Give it to Patrick O'Brien that excelled mightily at the bulleting. He'll eat it piecemeal like a dog. *(Mrs. O'Dea and Smith go out, and lock the door.)* We're all here, the gang of us, all the heroes of my youth, in these rooms, crying and imagining, or strung out like poor paste pearls of people along the rows of the grave-yard. Lizzie Moran and Dorothy Cullen I saw there, two beauties of Lathaleer, and Hannigan that killed his mother, under a whinbush. And the five daughters of Joseph Quinn, the five of them, much to my amazement, side by side in five short graves. All of them lost their wits and died, Black Jim. If I could lead those poor souls back across the meadows and the white lanes to the hearths and niches of their youth, and fill the farms with them again, with their hopes and dreams, by God … I am a tired old man and I'll have terrible aches forthwith. Let him hit. What else has he, but hitting? Does he know why the calf is stupid? No. There he is in his ignorance, hitting. Let him hit. *(After a little.)* My two bonny grandsons would cure me. *(After a little.)* It's a cold wind that blows without forgiveness, as the song says. *(There's a sort of darkness in the room now, with a*

seep of lights. Willie stands in the corner, quietly, singing softly.) My
poor son.... When I was a small child, smaller than yourself, my
Ma Ma brought me home a red fire engine from Baltinglass. It
was wrapped in the newspaper and hid in the hayshed for the
Christmas. But I knew every nook and cranny of the hayshed,
and I soon had it found, and the paper off it. And quite shortly
I had invented a grand game, where I stood one foot on the
engine and propelled myself across the yard. I kept falling and
falling, tearing and scumming my clothes, but no matter, the
game was a splendid game. And my mother she came out for
something, maybe to fling the grains at the hens in that
evening time, and she saw me skating on the engine and she
looked at me. She looked with a terrible long face, and I
looked down and there was the lovely engine all scratched and
bent, and the wheel half rubbed off it. So she took the toy quietly from under my foot, and marched over to the dunghill
and shoved it in deep with her bare hands, tearing at the rubbish there and the layers of dung. So I sought out her favourite
laying hen and put a yard-bucket over it, and it wasn't found
for a week, by which time the Christmas was over and the poor
hen's wits had gone astray from hunger and darkness and in-
ertia. Nor did it ever lay eggs again that quickened with chicks.
And that was a black time between my Ma Ma and me. *(After a
little.)* You were six when your Mam died, Willie. Hardly
enough time to be at war with her, the way a son might. She
was very attached to you. Her son. She had a special way of
talking about you, a special music in her voice. And she was
proud of your singing, and knew you could make a go of it, in
the halls, if you wished. I wanted to kill her when she said that.
But at six you sang like a linnet, true enough. *(After a little.)* I
didn't do as well as she did, with you. I was sorry you never
reached six feet. I was a fool. What big loud talking fools are
fathers sometimes. Why do we not love our sons simply and be
done with it? She did. I would kill, or I would do a great thing,
just to see you once more, in the flesh. All I got back was your
uniform, with the mud only half-washed out of it. Why do they
send the uniforms to the fathers and the mothers? I put it over
my head and cried for a night, like an owl in a tree. I cried for

41

a night with your uniform over my head, and no one saw me. *(Mrs. O'Dea unlocks the door and comes in with the new suit, a rough black suit that she has joined with her yellow thread. She brings it to his bedside, dispelling Willie.)*

MRS. O'DEA.   Look at the lovely thread I used in it, just like you asked. Do you think you are quiet now?

THOMAS.   Yes. *(Mrs. O'Dea starts to untie him, Smith comes in with a bowl of food, puts it on the table.)*

MRS. O'DEA.   *(To Smith.)* Help me get him into bed. He'll lie quiet. *(To Thomas.)* Take off the long johns too, I'll wash them for you. *(Smith pulls down the top. The two wounds from the beating are revealed on Thomas' chest.)* We should put something on those weals.

SMITH.   He's only scratched. Let the sleep heal him. He'll spring up in the morning, gabbling as always, crazy as ever. God knows I can't deal with him now, I have a fancy dress to go to in the town.

MRS. O'DEA.   Well, I can't wash a man, Mr. Smith.

SMITH.   He doesn't need washing. He's barely marked.

MRS. O'DEA.   Won't you at least wash his hands, they're all black from the floor. And I suppose his feet are as bad.

SMITH.   He may be St. Thomas, Mrs. O'Dea, but I'm not Jesus Christ, to be washing his hands and feet.

MRS. O'DEA.   What is he talking about, Mr. Dunne?

SMITH.   I have to collect my costume at six, Mrs. O'Dea, off the Dublin train.

MRS. O'DEA.   Tuck yourself up, Mr. Dunne, and have a rest. *(They go out. Annie and Dolly come on in mid-conversation.)*

DOLLY.   Where is my husband to come from, if we're to go back to Wicklow? I'm not marrying a farmer.

ANNIE.   Oh, are you not, Dolly? Isn't it pleasant to pick and choose? What farmer would take a woman like me, and I might have had a sailor once for a husband if I'd been let. So you're not the only one with difficulties, though you always think you are. That's the way of the pretty.

DOLLY.   You couldn't go marrying a sailor, Annie. You never see a sailor. They're always away — sailing.

ANNIE.   And our father humiliated by renegades. Collins!

DOLLY. They didn't humiliate him, Annie, indeed, not at all. I'm sure it was all very polite. I think the truth is, Papa is delighted to be going back to Kiltegan, where he can have us all about him, slaving for him, and being his good girls, and never never marrying.

ANNIE. Dolly, that's poor wickedness.

DOLLY. I know.

ANNIE. He's desolated to be going back.

DOLLY. I don't believe he is. Or he'd have taken the new post in the whatever you call them. The Civic Guard.

ANNIE. You don't think they were offering him Chief Superintendent?

DOLLY. So. Let him be a superintendent again, and stay in Dublin, where a person can buy a decent hat. There's nothing in Baltinglass but soda bread and eggs.

ANNIE. There's your father struggling to put a brave face on this day, which is no doubt the death of all good things for this country, and you're worrying about hats.

DOLLY. Hats are more dependable than countries.

ANNIE. You're a nonsensical girl, Dolly. Why don't you go away somewhere with yourself, if you don't want to go back to Wicklow?

DOLLY. I might!

ANNIE. You will not!

DOLLY. Aren't you just after telling me to?

ANNIE. Dolly, don't dream of going and leaving me alone in Wicklow!

DOLLY. For you to be giving out to me, like I was a little girl, and telling me I mustn't think of hats?

ANNIE. *(Seriously.)* Dolly, Dolly, you wouldn't go?

DOLLY. Why not?

ANNIE. *(Almost shaking her.)* Dolly, I'm serious, say you wouldn't. *(After a little.)* Say you wouldn't.

DOLLY. All right, all right, I wouldn't! I wouldn't. I wouldn't, Annie, dear. *(Annie nods at her fiercely. They go off.)*

THOMAS. *(From the bed.)* I could scarce get over the sight of him. He was a black-haired handsome man, but with the big face and body of a boxer. He would have made a tremendous

43

policeman in other days. He looked to me like Jack Dempsey, one of those prize-fighting men we admired. I would have been proud to have him as my son. When he walked he was sort of dancing, light on his pins, like a good bulleter. Like Patrick O'Brien himself. He looked like he might give Patrick O'Brien a good challenge for his money on some evening road somewhere, hoisting that ball of granite. He had glamour about him, like a man that goes about with the fit-ups, or one of those picture stars that came on the big ship from New York, to visit us, and there'd be crowds in the streets like for royalty, and it would be a fierce job to keep them held back. Big American men and women, twice the size of any Irish person. And some of them Irish too, but fed those many years on beef and wild turkeys. He was like that, Mr. Collins. I felt rough near him, that cold morning, rough, secretly. There never was enough gold in that uniform, never. I thought too as I looked at him of my father, as if Collins could have been my son and could have been my father. I had risen as high as a Catholic could go, and there wasn't enough braid, in the upshot. I remembered my father's anger when I failed at my schooling, and how he said he'd put me into the police, with the other fools of Ireland. I knew that by then most of the men in my division were for Collins, that they would have followed him wherever he wished, if he had called them. And for an instant, as the Castle was signed over to him, I felt a shadow of that loyalty pass across my heart. But I closed my heart instantly against it. We were to have peace. On behalf of the Crown the chief secretary wished him well. And indeed it was peaceful, that moment. The savagery and ruin that soon followed broke my heart again and again and again. My streets and squares became places for murder and fire. All that spring and summer, as now and then some brave boy spat at me in the streets, I could not hold back the tide of ruin. It was a personal matter. We had restored order in the days of Larkin. One morning I met a man in St. Stephen's Green. He was looking at a youngster thrown half-in under a bush. No more than eighteen. The man himself was one of that army of ordinary, middle-class Irishmen with firm views and moustaches. He was apoplectic.

We looked at each other. The birds were singing pleasantly, the early sun was up. "My grandsons," he said, "will be feral in this garden — mark my words." *(Dolly, Maud and Annie come on and move Thomas' table out a little and start to half-set it. There's a knock, and Matt appears.)*

ANNIE.   Who are you? What do you want?

DOLLY.   Who is that, Annie?

ANNIE.   What do you want here?

MATT.   My name's Matthew Kirwin, ma'am. I was asked to supper by Maud Dunne.

ANNIE.   By Maud Dunne?

MAUD.   *(Coming over.)* Oh, hello, Mr. Kirwin. How kind of you to come.

ANNIE.   How kind of him to come?

MAUD.   Come in, Mr. Kirwin, and meet my sisters. This is Dolly.

DOLLY.   How do you do?

MAUD.   And this is Annie.

ANNIE.   Yes, this is Annie. And who is this, Maud?

MAUD.   My friend, Annie, Mr. Matthew Kirwin.

ANNIE.   Since when do you have friends, Maud, coming to supper?

MAUD.   I suppose I can have friends just as soon as Dolly? I suppose I can.

ANNIE.   And have you known Mr. Kirwin long, Maud?

MAUD.   We have an acquaintance. Mr. Kirwin was painting in Stephen's Green last Saturday, and I happened to look over his shoulder at what he was doing, and as a matter of fact he was quite cross with me, weren't you, Mr. Kirwin, for doing so, and we fell to talking then, and I explained my interest in the old masters....

ANNIE.   Your interest in the old masters?

MAUD.   Yes, Annie. And we both agreed that the newer type of painters were all mad, and I invited him to supper.

ANNIE.   *(Almost pushing him back.)* I'm sorry, Mr. Kirwin, but you'll have to go.

MAUD.   Annie Dunne!

ANNIE.   I don't know how you got past the gates, but there

are to be no strangers coming in here. *(Pushing him elegantly.)*

MATT.   If it isn't convenient....

ANNIE.   It isn't even desirable, Mr. Kirwin.

MAUD.   Annie, lay your hands off that man, he is my artist that I found in Stephen's Green.

ANNIE.   And do you go out into the street, these times, Maud, and shake hands with everyone you see, and ask them to supper, if they are not doing anything better that night?

MAUD.   I do not, Annie Dunne.

ANNIE.   What do you know about a man like this, with the leisure to be painting in daylight....

MATT.   It was my day off, Miss Dunne....

ANNIE.   And with a foreign accent....

MATT.   I'm from Cork city....

ANNIE.   And who may be the greatest rogue or the greatest saint that ever came out of — Cork city....

MAUD.   You are not my mother, Annie, in fact I am older and wiser than you....

DOLLY.   Let him stay till Papa comes, Annie, and if Papa says he is all right, we can have him to supper. It would be lovely to have friends to supper again. Let's, Annie.

ANNIE.   And if he is an assassin?

DOLLY.   He's just a young man like any other young man.

ANNIE.   So are assassins. No, it cannot be. *(Pushing him more vigorously.)* Out with you, Mr. Kirwin.

MAUD.   Leave him be, oh, Annie, leave him be! *(She seems faint now, her legs buckling under her.)* Leave my artist be.... *(Dolly tries to hold her up.)*

DOLLY.   Help me, please. *(Matt holds her too.)*

ANNIE.   Let go of her, let go of her! *(Maud falls to the ground.)*

DOLLY.   Oh, Annie, look what you've done now. Now we're the assassins, and Maud is killed. *(The banging of a door below.)*

ANNIE.   That's Papa. Papa always bangs the lower door for us, Mr. Kirwin, because he has a house of girls. Now you'll get your supper!

MATT.   I assure you, Miss Dunne.... *(Thomas comes from the bed and stops by them. He doesn't speak. Maud opens her eyes, looks at him, gets up. Dolly goes and kisses her father.)*

DOLLY.   What is it, Papa? You look so pale.

MAUD.   Do you have a chill, Papa?

MATT.   *(To Annie.)* I'll go, I'll go....

ANNIE.   *(Not hearing him.)* Are you all right, Papa?

THOMAS.   *(After a little.)* The city is full of death. *(After a little, crying.)* The city is full of death.

ANNIE.   *(Hissing to Maud.)* Look at the state Papa is in — it's no night for a visitor.

THOMAS.   How do you do, how do you do.

MAUD.   *(To Matt.)* By the pillar, Saturday noon. *(Matt nods and goes.)*

THOMAS.   Do I smell a stew, a real stew? Is that the aroma of lamb, bless me?

ANNIE.   It is, Papa.

THOMAS.   Where did you get lamb, Annie?

ANNIE.   The Dunnes of Feddin sent it up. It's Wicklow lamb.

THOMAS.   Wicklow. It is — Elysium. It is paradise.... We'll be happy there, girls....

ANNIE.   We will, Papa. We'll fetch the supper, Papa. *(But they go out taking the things from the table with them. The door unlocks behind Thomas, and Smith enters with a basin and a bottle of ointment. He is dressed like a cowboy complete with six-shooters. Thomas stares at him.)*

THOMAS.   Black Jim!

SMITH.   Ah, never let it be said I left you alone with those cuts. Come here and sit, if you will. *(Thomas obediently goes to the stool. Smith puts down the bowl and begins to tend to Thomas.)* What's got into me? There's a lovely party going on in the town.

THOMAS.   I could be a man war-wounded.

SMITH.   You could. Or the outcome of a punch-up in a western saloon.

THOMAS.   *(Laughing.)* You think so?

SMITH.   *(Posing with the ointment.)* Do I not remind you of anyone in this get-up?

THOMAS.   *(Trying.)* No.

SMITH.   Maybe you never fancied the pictures, did you?

THOMAS.   I went the odd time to the magic lanthorn show.

47

SMITH. You couldn't guess then who I am, besides being Mr. Smith, I mean?

THOMAS. Black Jim?

SMITH. Gary Cooper, Gary Cooper. Ah, you're no use.

THOMAS. Gary Cooper? Is that the Coopers of Rathdangan?

SMITH. *(Putting on the ointment.)* Lilac Time. Did you never catch that? You haven't lived. Of course, it wasn't a cowboy as such. *Redemption* was a hell of a good cowboy.

THOMAS. No man is beyond redemption, my Ma Ma said, when he let the dog live.

SMITH. Who, Thomas? If men were beyond redemption, Thomas, what would we do in Ireland for Presidents?

THOMAS. That's a fair question. *(Laughing.)*

SMITH. *(Doing a cowboy.)* You dirty dog, you dirty dog. *(After a little.)* Did you go to the war, Thomas?

THOMAS. Me? No — I was too old. My son was with the Dublin Rifles.

SMITH. Oh, I think I knew that. He was the boy that was killed.

THOMAS. He was that boy.

SMITH. I had a first cousin in it. A lot of men went out.

THOMAS. Did he come home?

SMITH. Not at all. They sent the uniform.

THOMAS. That's right, they do. I've only a letter from him, that's all I have in the world of him.

SMITH. Written from the battlefield?

THOMAS. Oh, aye, from the trenches themselves.

SMITH. I'd be very interested to see that letter.

THOMAS. Would you, Mr. Smith? Of course. I have it some-where, stuck in Annie's book. Will I get it?

SMITH. Do, get it, man, and we'll have a read of it. Why not?

THOMAS. *(Fetching the letter.)* Do you not want to get to your fancy dress?

SMITH. The party can wait. *(Taking the old letter.)* It looks old enough.

THOMAS. Well, it's coming up to twenty year ago now.

SMITH. *(Opening it carefully.)* It's an historical document.

THOMAS. *(Laughing.)* Oh, aye. Historical.

SMITH. *(Reading.)* He has a good hand at the writing, anyhow. *(Reading.)*

THOMAS. *(Nudging his knee.)* Would you not....

SMITH. Read it aloud? You want me to?

THOMAS. I do. I would greatly like that.

SMITH. Fair enough. Okay. *(Settling himself to read it, clearing his voice, a little self-conscious.)* Of course, I don't read aloud much, so.... *(Thomas smiles.)* Right. — My dearest Papa, Here I am writing to you in the midst of all these troubles. We are three weeks now in the one spot and we all feel we are dug in here for an eternity. The shells going over have become familiar to us, and my friend the first lieutenant from Leitrim, Barney Miles, has given our regular rats names. Our first idea was to thump them with spades because they eat the corpses up on the field but surely there has been enough death. We have not got it as bad as some companies, because our position is raised, and we get drainage, but all the same we know what real mud is by now. We have had some miracles, in that last week deep in the night one of our men was thrown back over the rampart wounded, by what hands we do not know. Another man was sent out with a dispatch and on his way back found a big sow thrashing in the mud. He would have taken her on with him for chops except she was twice his weight and not keen. It made us remember that all hereabout was once farms, houses and farms and grass and stock, and surely the farmer in you would weep, Papa, to see the changes. I hope you don't mind my letter going on. It gives me great comfort to write to my father. You will probably think I am raving a bit, and ranting, but nevertheless, since I am so far distant, I tell myself you will be interested to get news of me here. I wish I could tell you that I am a hero, but truth to tell, there are few opportunities for valour, in the way we all imagined when we set out. I have not seen the enemy. Sometimes in the dark and still of the nighttimes I see lights over where their position is, and on the stillest evenings you can just hear their voices. Sometimes they sing! Sometimes we sing, low and quiet, we have quite a repertoire now of risky songs, that you wouldn't approve at all. But it is a grand thing that we can still use our voices, and when I sing I think of home, and my sisters, and my father, and hope and know that my mother is watching over me here. God keep you all safe, because we have been told of the ruckus at home, and some of the country men are as much upset by that as they would be by their present emergency. I know you are in the front line there, Papa, so keep yourself safe for my return, when Maud will cook the fatted calf! The plain truth is, Papa, this is a strange war and a strange time, and my whole wish is to be home with you all in Dublin, and to abide by your wishes, whatever they be. I wish to be a more dutiful son because, Papa, in the mire of this wasteland, you stand before my eyes as the finest man I know, and in my dreams you comfort me, and keep my spirits lifted. Your son, Willie.

THOMAS. *(After a little while, Smith folds the letter and gives it back to him.)* In my dreams you comfort me....

SMITH. That's a beautiful letter, Mr. Dunne. A memento. A keepsake. *(Thomas nods his head, thinking. Getting up to go.)* Good man, good man. *(Goes, locks the door. Thomas puts away his letter and climbs into bed. After a little Dolly enters and goes to his bedside, with a big ticket in her hand. Thomas looks at her, takes the ticket, reads it, looks at her.)*

DOLLY. You aren't angry, Papa? It took all my courage to buy it, every ounce I had, you can't imagine. *(After a little.)* You are wondering how I could afford it? It was quite expensive, but it's only steerage. I had to sell Mam's bracelet that I was given, the ruby one you gave me, and I've to work for an agency the first two years, as a domestic, in Cleveland, Ohio.

THOMAS. *(After a little.)* Is it because she died on us? She was mortally sorry to die. She died as the need for candlelight failed. She would have adored you, even as she gave her life for you.

DOLLY. Papa, don't be angry with me, please, I could not bear it, it took all my courage.

THOMAS. Why would you go, Dolly, that is loved by us all, and young men going crazy over you here, and queuing up to marry you?

DOLLY. They're not, Papa. I want to be liked and loved, but people are cold towards me, Papa.

THOMAS. Why would they be, Dolly?

DOLLY. Because — because of you, Papa, I suppose.

THOMAS. It will pass, Dolly. In Wicklow we will be among our own people.

DOLLY. I don't want to be like the Dunnes of Feddin, three wild women with unkept hair and slits on the backs of their hands from ploughing. You're old, Papa, it's not the same for you.

THOMAS. *(Smiling, giving back the ticket.)* Yes, I am old.

DOLLY. I didn't mean to say that, Papa. I knew you would be angry with me, I prayed you wouldn't be.

THOMAS. Come here to me. *(He embraces her.)* How could I be angry with you? It's a poor look-out if I am angry with my own baby because she is afraid.

DOLLY. I didn't want to hurt you, Papa.

THOMAS. Papa is strong enough for all these things.

DOLLY. You'll take care, Papa, and write to me, about all the goings-on in Kiltegan?

THOMAS. I will of course. *(The lock turns in the door, Dolly breaks from him, goes.)* I will of course! *(Mrs. O'Dea pops in and places a pair of black shoes by his bed.)*

MRS. O'DEA. I'm just putting these here for you. I found you shoes at last, to go with the beautiful suit. I didn't mean to disturb you. You're the neatest sleeper I ever did meet, Mr. Dunne. Never a ruffle in the sheets, just a long warm nest where your body lies.

THOMAS. That's about the height of it.

MRS. O'DEA. Oh, you're a man for a bit of philosophy, I know.

THOMAS. Whose shoes were they, Mrs. O'Dea?

MRS. O'DEA. Let's see now. They were Patrick O'Brien's, Mr. Dunne.

THOMAS. *(After a moment.)* You must take them for another man. I'd never fill them.

MRS. O'DEA. But what if your grandsons come to see you and you've nothing to put on your feet?

THOMAS. There's no chance of that now.

MRS. O'DEA. *(Taking up the bowl of food.)* It's stone cold and you ate nothing. *(Going.)* Didn't I make you a beautiful suit? *(She goes, locks the door. Annie comes on with one of his big socks to darn and sits on the stool and works on the darning. Thomas dons Mrs. O'Dea's suit.)*

ANNIE.   Three days now, Papa.

THOMAS.   Three days, Annie. And we'll be set up in the old house again. We'll get that dairy going again first thing, a good scrub-down with the carbolic.

ANNIE.   Yes.

THOMAS.   And I'll have our milking cow fetched over from Feddin, and the Dunnes of Feddin can hire someone else's fields, because we'll need them presently.

ANNIE.   We will.

THOMAS.   And we'll be dog tired every night from the wealth of work, and be proud. And we have eight Rhode Island Reds and a crowing cock, that they are keeping for me in Lathaleer. And they're looking out for a pony, they say they know a fair-minded tinker will sell us something apt, and two hours at the most with a pot of polish will have those high lamps on the old trap gleaming. And we will cut a fine figure, you and I, Annie, Thomas Dunne and his daughter, throughout Kiltegan, Feddin and Kelsha.

ANNIE.   We'll enjoy ourselves.

THOMAS.   And I'll lime the whole place. The house will be blinding white. We'll have red geraniums on the sills like the very dark conscience of summer or we're not Christians at all.

ANNIE.   And Maud to visit, and we'll be peering at her, you know? *(Winking.)*

THOMAS.   And letters from Dolly, in the meantime, till she wishes to come home. *(A knocking. The Recruit, now a constable, comes on. Annie goes to him. The Constable whispers in her ear. Annie comes back to Thomas.)*

ANNIE.   It's one of the constables, Papa. He wants a word with you privately. *(Thomas goes over to him. The Constable whispers to him. Thomas at length pats the man briefly on the arm. The Constable goes. Thomas returns slowly to Annie.)* What, Papa?

THOMAS.   They have killed Collins in Cork.

ANNIE.   *(After a little.)* We'll be doubly glad to be going home

now, and free of it all, Papa. *(Thomas can say nothing.)* Doubly glad. *(A country music, and the wide ash-glow of a fire in the grate.)*
THOMAS. *(To himself.)* She died as many persons do, at the death of candlelight, as the birds begin to sing. She was a child again at the end, as if she was back again years ago in Lathaleer, and talking to her father, Cullen the coppicer. I stood by her bed, holding Dolly in my arms like a three-pound bag of loose corn, and Cissy spoke to me as if I were her own father. But our account was clear. *(Calling.)* Annie! When I went out that day to stop Larkin in Sackville Street, all the world of my youth, the world of Ireland that I knew, was still in place, loyal, united and true. I had three lovely daughters, and a little son as glad as a rose. And I had risen as high as Catholic could in the Dublin Metropolitan Police. And we were drawn up, ready to dispel them. *(Sits in near fire.)* Annie!
ANNIE. Yes, Papa?
THOMAS. Bring my sword, would you?
ANNIE. No, Papa, I'm not bringing your sword.
THOMAS. There's fellas roaming the countryside seeking out the maiming of this man and the death of that man, old scores must be settled, they're whispering and conspiring in the dark.
ANNIE. There's nothing and no one out there, Papa.
THOMAS. But there is. I can smell them. Dark boys in black suits bought off the back of carts in county fairs, with old guns that might as soon blow off their own fingers when they fire. They won't get us. You must bring the sword.
ANNIE. There's nothing but your own fears. Go in to your bed and pull the blankets over your face and get a sleep, Papa.
THOMAS. And lose my last daughter to ruffians and murderers?
ANNIE. You have the respect of the district, Papa.
THOMAS. And what about that filthy mass of men that came up the yard last week and rattled our latch, and shouted in at me, while you were away at the well?
ANNIE. It was only a crowd of tinkers, Papa, that thought you were a woman alone, and wanted to frighten you. They took two churns from the shed and a length of rope because you wouldn't go out to them.

53

THOMAS. I didn't dare breathe, I didn't dare breathe. I held fast to the fire.

ANNIE. Papa, you know country life better than me, but you are not suited to it, I think. *(A soughing in the maples outside.)*

THOMAS. There's them breathing now. Fetch the sword! *(The soughing. Thomas bolts from the stool and gets the sword, comes back and stands in the middle of the room holding it high.)* Come in now to us, and see what you'll get!

ANNIE. Papa, Papa, please. *(She tries to hold him and take the sword.)* If you'll be quiet, I'll make us another pot of tea and then we can go to our rest.

THOMAS. *(Breaking from her.)* I must strike, I must strike. *(He goes about hitting at whatever he can, table and stool and such.)* Look at them running about like rats! Annie, there's rats come in, down the chimney! *(Striking the floor.)* Look at them, they're too quick for me!

ANNIE. There's no rats in my house! *(She covers her face with her hands.)* It's a clean house.

THOMAS. *(Raving.)* What a to-do and a turmoil it is, with all their heroes lying in state about the city! They're bringing him up tonight to lie in state in the Pro-cathedral! Collins! We'll be doubly glad to be going home, now, she said! Because of you, Papa, I suppose, says Dolly. Says Dolly, says Dolly, says Dolly, says Dolly....

ANNIE. Papa! Stop it! *(He does. He stands still where he is, the sword loose in his grip. He breathes heavily. He sinks to his knees, offers Annie the sword.)*

THOMAS. Please, child....

ANNIE. What now?

THOMAS. I am quiet now, Annie. I ask you a simple favour.

ANNIE. What favour, Papa?

THOMAS. Take the sword, Annie, and raise it up like a slash-hook, and bring it down on top of me like I was brambles, with all your might. *(Annie looks at him. She goes to him and pulls the sword roughly from him. Maybe she considers using it for a moment. She goes, taking the sword with her. Thomas stares after her. He closes his eyes and cries like a child. The fire fades away, and the colder light of his room in the Baltinglass home returns. Willie comes, his uniform*

54

flecked with gold. Thomas' head down.) Da Da, Ma Ma, Ba Ba....
(After a little, seeing his son.) Oh, Willie.... *(Humorously.)* The
great appear great because we are on our knees. Let us rise.
*(Willie holds out a hand to help him get up. Thomas is surprised to
find it solid enough when he takes it.)* Oh, Willie.... *(Willie brings
him over to the bed and helps him get in.)* It's all topsy-turvy, Willie.
(After a little.) Sure, Willie, I think the last order I gave to the
men was to be sure and salute Mr. Collins' coffin as it went
by.... *(After a little.)* One time, Willie, and it was Christmastime
too, and I was a young fellow in Kiltegan, our dog Shep went
missing for some days, as dogs in winter will. I was maybe ten
or eleven, and I loved that Shep, and feared he was gone forever. We had got him as a young dog that had been beaten
somewhere, and broken, till he reached our haven, and un-
coiled, and learned to bark like a baby learns to laugh, and he
shone at his work. *(Willie gets up on the bed beside his father.)* One
morning early after a fall of snow I went out to break the ice
on the rain-barrel to plash my face, and I saw his tracks in the
snow going up the sloping field, high to the fringes of the
wood, and I was greatly afeared, because there were drops of
blood now and then as he went, little smears of it on the
cleanly snow. So I followed him up, sinking here and there in
the drifts, well used to it, well used to it, and on a piece of field
we called the upper garden, because it was flat there and you
could see across to Baltinglass and some said even to Shillelagh
and the dark woods of Coollattin, I found our dog there with
the carcass of a ewe well-eaten, only the hindquarters remain-
ing. I saw my father's blue sign on the wool and knew the
worst. For a dog that would kill a sheep would die himself. So
in my innocence I went down to my father and told him and
he instructed me, as was right and proper, to go back up with
a rope and lead Shep down so the killing could take place. The
loss of a ewe was a disaster, a disaster, there'd be pounds of
money gone into her. But I loved the dog so sorely, I hesitated
when I had the rope tied about him, and at length led him off
further up the hill, across the little stand of scrubby pines, and
on into the low woods dark with snow and moss. And we went
through by a snaking path I knew, till we got to the other side,

where there was a simple man living, that made his living from the rabbits, and maybe had need of a watchful dog. But he wouldn't take a dog that had killed, though he was a tender man enough, and it behoved me to retrace my steps back into the woods, now moving along but slowly, and the dog sort of dragging behind, as if he knew well his misdeed and his fate. And I stopped in the centre of the trees, and do you know my young legs would not go forward, they would not proceed, try as I might, and there I was all that afternoon and night with the dog and the hazels. How is it that the drear of winter didn't eat my bones and murder me for my foolishness? Love of the dog kept me standing there, as only a child can stand, without moving, thinking, the poor dog whimpering with the cold. About five o'clock I went on, because I heard calling over the hill, here and there, and I could see black figures with lights moving and calling, calling out to me and the dog to come home. We came down the sloping field with the neighbours about us, them not saying a word, maybe marvelling at me, thinking I had been dead, and the torches and lamps making everything crazy with light, the old crab apple enlarging to the size of the field, its branches wild like arms. Down at last into the yard we came, the dog skulking on the rope just the same as the day he had arrived to us, and my father came out from the house in his big clothes. All brown with clothes and hair. It was as if I had never seen him in his entirety, from head to toe. And I knew then that the dog and me were for slaughter. My feet carried me on to where he stood, immortal you would say in the door. And he put his right hand on the back of my head, and pulled me to him so that my cheek rested against the buckle of his belt. And he raised his own face to the brightening sky and praised someone, in a crushed voice, God maybe, for my safety, and stroked my hair. And the dog's crime was never spoken of, but that he lived till he died. And I would call that the mercy of fathers, when the love that lies in them deeply like the glittering face of a well is betrayed by an emergency, and the child sees at last that he is loved, loved and needed and not to be lived without, and greatly. *(He sleeps. Willie lies in close to him. Sleeps. Music. Dark.)*

PROPERTY LIST

Key (MRS. O'DEA, SMITH)
Basin (SMITH)
Tape measure (MRS. O'DEA)
Ragged socks (THOMAS)
Cracked bowl with stew (SMITH)
Big spoon (SMITH, THOMAS)
White shirt (ANNIE)
Dress uniform (MAUDE)
Ceremonial sword (MAUDE, THOMAS)
Polished boots (DOLLY)
Pacifier (baton) (SMITH)
Newspaper (SMITH)
Chamber pot (SMITH)
Big flaps of black cloth (MRS. O'DEA)
Pins (MRS. O'DEA)
Bobbin (MRS. O'DEA)
Pin (THOMAS)
Bundle of socks (ANNIE)
Square-cut cardboard (MATT)
Handbag (ANNIE)
Brown paper bag with bunch of heather (ANNIE)
Book (THOMAS)
Pillow (THOMAS)
Helmet
White rose buttonhole (DOLLY)
Strait-jacket (MRS. O'DEA)
Bowl of food (SMITH)
Black suit of clothes, with yellow stitching (MRS. O'DEA)
Bottle of ointment (SMITH)
Letter (THOMAS)
Ticket (DOLLY)
Pair of black shoes (MRS. O'DEA)
Sock and darning material (ANNIE)

NEW PLAYS

• **MERE MORTALS by David Ives, author of *All in the Timing*.** Another critically acclaimed evening of one-act comedies combining wit, satire, hilarity and intellect -- a winning combination. The entire evening of plays can be performed by 3 men and 3 women. ISBN: 0-8222-1632-9

• **BALLAD OF YACHIYO by Philip Kan Gotanda.** A provocative play about innocence, passion and betrayal, set against the backdrop of a Hawaiian sugar plantation in the early 1900s. *"Gotanda's writing is superb ... a great deal of fine craftsmanship on display here, and much to enjoy."* --Variety. *"...one of the country's most consistently intriguing playwrights..."* --San Francisco Examiner. *"As he has in past plays, Gotanda defies expectations..."* --Oakland Tribune. [3M, 4W] ISBN: 0-8222-1547-0

• **MINUTES FROM THE BLUE ROUTE by Tom Donaghy.** While packing up a house, a family converges for a weekend of flaring tempers and shattered illusions. *"With MINUTES FROM THE BLUE ROUTE [Donaghy] succeeds not only in telling a story -- a typically American one with wide appeal, about how parents and kids struggle to understand each other and mostly fail -- but in notating it inventively, through wittily elliptical, crisscrossed speeches, and in making it carry a fairly vast amount of serious weight with surprising ease."* --Village Voice. [2M, 2W] ISBN: 0-8222-1608-6

• **SCAPIN by Molière, adapted by Bill Irwin and Mark O'Donnell.** This adaptation of Molière's 325-year-old farce, *Les Fourberies de Scapin*, keeps the play in period while adding a late Twentieth Century spin to the language and action. *"This SCAPIN, [with a] felicitous adaptation by Mark O'Donnell, would probably have gone over big with the same audience who first saw Molière's Fourberies de Scapin...in Paris in 1671."* --N.Y. Times. *"Commedia dell'arte and vaudeville have at least two things in common: baggy pants and Bill Irwin. All make for a natural fit in the celebrated clown's entirely unconventional adaptation."* --Variety [9M, 3W, flexible] ISBN: 0-8222-1603-5

• **THE TURN OF THE SCREW adapted for the stage by Jeffrey Hatcher from the story by Henry James.** The American master's classic tale of possession is given its most interesting "turn" yet: one woman plays the mansion's terrified governess while a single male actor plays everyone else. *"In his thoughtful adaptation of Henry James' spooky tale, Jeffrey Hatcher does away with the supernatural flummery, exchanging the story's balanced ambiguities about the nature of reality for a portrait of psychological vampirism..."* --Boston Globe. [1M, 1W] ISBN: 0-8222-1554-3

• **NEVILLE'S ISLAND by Tim Firth.** A middle management orientation exercise turns into an hilarious disaster when the team gets "shipwrecked" on an uninhabited island. *"NEVILLE'S ISLAND ... is that rare event: a genuinely good new play..., it's a comedic, adult LORD OF THE FLIES..."* --The Guardian. *"... A non-stop, whitewater deluge of comedy both sophisticated and slapstick.... Firth takes a perfect premise and shoots it to the extreme, flipping his fish out of water, watching them flop around a bit, and then masterminding the inevitable feeding frenzy."* --New Mexican. [4M] ISBN: 0-8222-1581-0

DRAMATISTS PLAY SERVICE, INC.
440 Park Avenue South, New York, NY 10016 212-683-8960 Fax 212-213-1539
postmaster@dramatists.com www.dramatists.com

NEW PLAYS

• **TAKING SIDES by Ronald Harwood.** Based on the true story of one of the world's greatest conductors whose wartime decision to remain in Germany brought him under the scrutiny of a U.S. Army determined to prove him a Nazi. *"A brave, wise and deeply moving play delineating the confrontation between culture, and power, between art and politics, between irresponsible freedom and responsible compromise." --London Sunday Times.* [4M, 3W] ISBN: 0-8222-1566-7

• **MISSING/KISSING by John Patrick Shanley.** Two biting short comedies, MISSING MARISA and KISSING CHRISTINE, by one of America's foremost dramatists and the Academy Award winning author of *Moonstruck*. *" ... Shanley has an unusual talent for situations ... and a sure gift for a kind of inner dialogue in which people talk their hearts as well as their minds...." --N.Y. Post.* MISSING MARISA [2M], KISSING CHRISTINE [1M, 2W] ISBN: 0-8222-1590-X

• **THE SISTERS ROSENSWEIG by Wendy Wasserstein, Pulitzer Prize-winning author of *The Heidi Chronicles*.** Winner of the 1993 Outer Critics Circle Award for Best Broadway Play. A captivating portrait of three disparate sisters reuniting after a lengthy separation on the eldest's 50th birthday. *"The laughter is all but continuous." --New Yorker. "Funny. Observant. A play with wit as well as acumen.... In dealing with social and cultural paradoxes, Ms. Wasserstein is, as always, the most astute of commentators." --N.Y. Times.* [4M, 4W] ISBN: 0-8222-1348-6

• **MASTER CLASS by Terrence McNally. Winner of the 1996 Tony Award for Best Play.** Only a year after winning the Tony Award for *Love! Valour! Compassion!*, Terrence McNally scores again with the most celebrated play of the year, an unforgettable portrait of Maria Callas, our century's greatest opera diva. *"One of the white-hot moments of contemporary theatre. A total triumph." --N.Y. Post. "Blazingly theatrical." -- USA Today.* [3M, 3W] ISBN: 0-8222-1521-7

• **DEALER'S CHOICE by Patrick Marber.** A weekly poker game pits a son addicted to gambling against his own father, who also has a problem but won't admit it. *"... make tracks to DEALER'S CHOICE, Patrick Marber's wonderfully masculine, razor-sharp dissection of poker-as-life.... It's a play that comes out swinging and never lets up -- a witty, wisecracking drama that relentlessly probes the tortured souls of its six very distinctive ... characters. CHOICE is a cutthroat pleasure that you won't want to miss." --Time Out (New York).* [6M] ISBN: 0-8222-1616-7

• **RIFF RAFF by Laurence Fishburne.** RIFF RAFF marks the playwriting debut of one of Hollywood's most exciting and versatile actors. *"Mr. Fishburne is surprisingly and effectively understated, with scalding bubbles of anxiety breaking through the surface of a numbed calm." --N.Y. Times. "Fishburne has a talent and a quality...[he] possesses one of the vital requirements of a playwright -- a good ear for the things people say and the way they say them." --N.Y. Post.* [3M] ISBN: 0-8222-1545-4

DRAMATISTS PLAY SERVICE, INC.
440 Park Avenue South, New York, NY 10016 212-683-8960 Fax 212-213-1539
postmaster@dramatists.com www.dramatists.com